BRANCH LINES OF EAST LONDON

J.E. CONNOR

MP Middleton Press

LMSR Class 3F 0-6-0T No. 7301 heads east through Hackney station with a coal train in the 1930s. A covered footway connected the west end of the platforms with Hackney Downs station on the former GER, and the large board seen to the right of the locomotive advised passengers to change if they wish to use this facility to reach trains for Chingford, Enfield or Palace Gates. (Lens of Sutton)

First published February 2000

ISBN 1 901706 44 3

© Middleton Press

Cover design Deborah Esher

Published by
  Middleton Press
  Easebourne Lane
  Midhurst, West Sussex
  GU29 9AZ
Tel: 01730 813169
Fax: 01730 812601

Layout and typesetting London Railway Record

Printed & bound by Biddles Ltd.
  Guildford and Kings Lynn

CONTENTS

Modern stations are included in brackets.

1-42   Stepney East to Blackwall and North
        Greenwich *(Limehouse, Mudchute,
        Island Gardens)*

43-54   Bow Road

55-120 Dalston Junction to Poplar (East
        India Road) *(Hackney Central,
        Homerton and Bow Chuch to
        All Saints)*

INDEX

119 All Saints
29   Blackwall
89   Bow
99   Bow Church
43   Bow Road
101 Bow Works
55   Dalston Junction
110 Devons Road
107 Devons Road Locomotive Depot
58   Graham Road Goods Depot
60   Hackney Central
74   Hackney Wick Goods Depot
120 Harrow Lane Goods Office
68   Homerton
42   Island Gardens
5   Limehouse

1   Limehouse (formerly Stepney East)
4   Limehouse Junction
33   Millwall Docks
36   Millwall Park Viaduct
15   Millwall Junction
35   Mudchute
38   North Greenwich & Cubitt Town
83   Old Ford
23   Poplar
116 Poplar (East India Road)
111 South Bromley
32   South Dock
75   Victoria Park
10   Westferry
11   West India Docks

ACKNOWLEDGEMENTS

Sadly, only a few photographers recorded the magnificent complex of lines which once served London's East End, but to those whose valuable work has made this volume possible, I would like to express my heartfelt thanks. Amongst these, I feel special mention should be made of my good friend, the late Bob Cogger, who back in the early 1950s, travelled around not just this area, but other parts of his beloved London, capturing much on film which would have otherwise been lost. Bob was a railwayman, and had permission to visit many places which were not accessible to the general public, so I believe a number of his views included in this album are unique.

Thanks are also due to Tricia and Barbie for assistance in checking the proofs, and my son Charlie for drawing the map which appears on page V.

GEOGRAPHICAL SETTING

All the lines featured herein are on the fairly level ground of the northern flood plain of the River Thames. Much of the railway route was built across marshland on a series of brick arches, although some of the area had already been reclaimed and converted to docks.

The Ordnance Survey maps are to the scale of 25 ins to 1 mile, unless otherwise stated.

III

HISTORICAL BACKGROUND

The lines which we will be looking at in this album may have been constructed by different companies, but throughout their existence they have shared similar fates. They were built at a time when the district immediately to the east of London was beginning to develop, and prospered until competition from other forms of transport began to take away much of their former patronage. As a result, they eventually lost their passenger services, and in time, road hauliers killed off the remaining freight traffic.

The lines then became derelict, and looked as if their formations would disappear beneath new developments, but fortunately this was not to be.

With the roads becoming ever more choked with traffic, it was obvious that something had to be done to improve travelling conditions around the capital, and the 1980s saw a revitalised interest in the railway network.

Sections of all three lines were eventually brought back into public use, and it is again possible to travel over them by train. Before we begin to explore them however, let us take a brief look at their history, and the companies which built them.

THE LONDON & BLACKWALL RAILWAY

By the early nineteenth century, the Thames was becoming extremely congested with river traffic, as ships and smaller craft made their way to and from the various docks which had been constructed within the London area. A new thoroughfare known as Commercial Road was constructed to link the docks at Poplar with the City, but this did little to improve matters, and in 1825 a proposal was made to lay an iron tramway along its full length. This failed to materialise, but between 1827 and 1829 a stone 'tramway' formed of parallel slabs of Aberdeen granite was installed instead.

All carts using this had to have their wheels set to an appropriate gauge, and tolls were levied, but although matters were slightly improved, it soon became obvious that the answer to the problem would be a railway.

Two different schemes were promoted, and on 28th July 1836, one of these received Parliamentary authority to proceed. Part of its length was to adjoin the south side of Commercial Road, so appropriately it was named 'The Commercial Railway'.

As there was no intention of joining it to any other lines which might be built in future, a non-standard track gauge of around 5ft was chosen, but this was not to be its only idiosyncrasy. Because the Commercial Railway's viaduct would lie alongside the Regent's Canal Dock, with its often inflammable cargoes, the idea of locomotive haulage had to be ruled out and an alternative found. It was felt that steam locos departing from the closely-spaced stations would emit sparks, and therefore cause fires in the wooden ships moored nearby. The decision was therefore taken to install stationary winding engines at either end, and pull the carriages by means of ropes.

The Commercial Railway was authorised to run westwards from Blackwall, but unfortunately, the City Fathers had no intention of it encroaching into their exclusive square mile. Therefore the line was forced to terminate at a less-than convenient terminus in the Minories. However, negotiations continued, and when the work was nearly completed, an extension into Fenchurch Street was authorised in 1839.

At the same time, the company title was changed to the London & Blackwall Railway, and as this, it was ceremonially opened on 4th July 1840.

As it was chiefly intended as a fast means of communication between the docks and City, the means of propulsion, on paper at least, was no disadvantage. However, in reality, the ropes initially used proved unsuitable, and breakages regularly caused problems. On one such occasion, it is recorded that a train was delayed for a lengthy time near West India Dock station, and the passengers, mainly young seamen returning to their ship, amused themselves by playing snowballs on the track!

The method of operating during the rope-hauled period was ingenious for its time and, when all was working properly, provided the world with its first true rapid transit system. Unfortunately, space does not permit a detailed description of operations, but basically, at the start of traffic, there was a train of about six coaches at either terminus. At the same time, individual vehicles would be standing at each intermediate station. At the appropriate time, a telegraph signal would be sent from one end of the line to the other, and the two stationery engines would be set in motion simultaneously, drawing the carriages towards it. As the complete trains reached their first intermediate station, the rear vehicle would be 'slipped', and brought to a stand by the 'brakesman' on board. This situation would continue until the opposite end of the line, until only one, or possibly two carriages were left coupled to the rope. These would be preceded into the terminus by coaches from the intermediate stations, and in this way, a new complete train would be made up. In the meantime, the vehicles dropped off on the journey waited at their appropriate stations until the cycle started again.

If passengers wished to travel from the Minories to Blackwall or vice-versa, the idea was fine, but journeys between two intermediate stations could only be carried out via one of the termini.

The short extension into Fenchurch Street was opened on 2nd August 1841, but even at this early stage, public patronage was not all it could have been. Because of the roundabout means of travelling from one intermediate station to another, passengers began to desert the railway, and revert to the less efficient, but more convenient horse drawn omnibuses, which plodded slowly along Commercial Road.

In addition to providing a useful link for commerce, the line provided an easy means of travelling from central London to Blackwall, where passengers could board ships, either purely for pleasure, or else for journeys to far off shores. Although the majority of these vessels either started or ended their voyages further upstream,

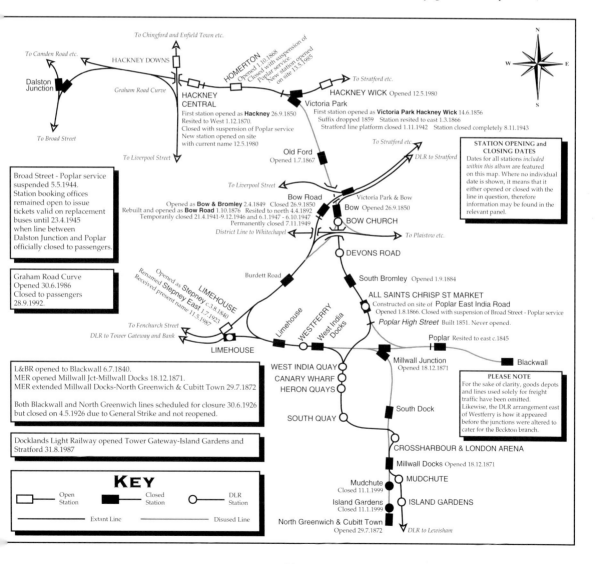

the stretch of river which curved around the pendulous Isle of Dogs peninsular was invariably extremely busy, and in bad weather could even be dangerous.

Although the formation of the LBR was double throughout, the means of operation meant that both tracks were worked singularly, so conventional Up and Down terminology did not apply. Instead, the track, which on a conventional railway would have been described as being on the Up side was known as 'The South Line', whilst the other was called 'The North Line'.

Improved cables were eventually employed, but it was obvious that the London & Blackwall was fast becoming a curiosity, as more conventional railways began to appear elsewhere. The company therefore decided to change its system to the standard gauge of 4ft 8$\frac{1}{2}$ins, and apply for authority to operate services with locomotives. This, together with a connecting line from a new junction at Stepney to the Eastern Counties Railway at Bow, was authorised by Acts of 1845 and 1846, but the work was not completed until three years later.

The idea of running steam locomotives alongside the Regent's Canal Dock was still thought unsafe however, so the company were obliged to cover the adjoining length of viaduct with a light iron roof to avoid the danger of stray sparks.

The end of cable haulage came on 14th February 1849, and following this, the redundant equipment on the 'South Line' was disconnected. From the same date, locomotives began working a forty-minute interval service on the 'North Line', and normal Up and Down running commenced using both tracks in early April.

At first, the line towards Bow, known officially as The London & Blackwall Extension Railway, or by its abbreviated form of The Blackwall Extension Railway, failed to come up to expectations, and was soon losing money. Whilst construction was still under way, the Eastern Counties Railway objected to the proposed junction between its own metals and those of the L&BR, and refused to allow a permanent physical connection between the two lines. This drastically cut down the route's potential, and the Blackwall company's trains were obliged to terminate at an exchange station called Victoria Park & Bow, which was tucked away in Fairfield Road.

It was not long before things began to look up however, as in September 1850, the East & West India Docks & Birmingham Junction Railway

(which became the North London Railway in 1853) opened its route from Islington to Bow, and thence over the L&BR into Fenchurch Street. With the new service up and running, the London & Blackwall no longer felt justified in operating its own trains over this route, so promptly withdrew them.

The frosty relationship between the ECR and the L&BR eventually thawed, although not before Parliamentary intervention. In April 1854, the first section of the London Tilbury & Southend Railway was opened, and made use of the junction at Bow, which had finally been installed.

After this, traffic on the Blackwall Extension line began to seriously increase, with the LTSR and NLR trains being joined by those of the ECR, which had also started using Fenchurch Street.

With all this happening, the original L&BR 'main line' between Stepney and Blackwall started to decline in importance, and eventually took on the status of a branch.

The ECR became part of the newly formed Great Eastern Railway in 1862, and the new company acquired the London & Blackwall system on a 999 year lease four years later.

As early as the 1870s, the GER began pondering the affects that tramway competition would have on the Blackwall line, and although perhaps a little premature, they were right to do so.

Following electrification of the tramways in the first decade of the twentieth century, the passenger figures on Blackwall branch services plummeted, and from 4th October 1908, its Sunday trains were withdrawn.

Nevertheless, they continued to operate throughout the remainder of the week, and although running around every fifteen minutes, there was little demand. In one of his books, the late Sir John Betjeman recalled that they were *"quite empty"*, and that the First Class compartments were so rarely used that they smelt like an old family brougham, which had lain forgotten in a stable.

The service survived World War 1, but the inevitable closure was announced in 1926. The notices were posted on 23rd March that year, showing a withdrawal date of 30th June, but because of industrial action during the General Strike, passenger trains ceased to run after 3rd May, and were never reinstated.

Freight traffic continued, but by the 1960s even this had been reduced to a trickle. Little use was

made of the line after 1962, and official aban-
donment came four years later.

THE MILLWALL EXTENSION RAILWAY

A branch linking the London & Blackwall
Railway with the Isle of Dogs was first suggest-
ed by the LBR directors in the Summer of 1863,
but their Bill was refused the necessary
Parliamentary authority. Until this time, the area
through which the intended line was to run consisted largely of desolate swamps, and had once
been known as 'Stepney Marsh'. Things began to
change with the development of the docks however, and the Company's intention was to get its
branch built before the price of land rose any
higher. With this in mind, the directors again
applied for permission to proceed, and this time
their application fortunately met with a positive
response. On 19th June 1865, an Act was passed
which sanctioned its construction, and the
scheme became known as 'The London,
Blackwall & Millwall Extension Railway'.

The branch was designed to leave the main line
at a junction near Harrow Lane, Poplar, then run
southwards to a riverside terminus in Johnson
Street, which was about 200 yards from a jetty
used by the Greenwich ferries. These had a long
history, which in fact dated back to 1550, when
King Edward VI originally authorised their operation. From 1676 onwards, the boats had been
provided by a company known as the Potter's
Ferry Society. However, in the early nineteenth
century these were joined by others which
worked a statutory service for horses and vehicles, created by the passing of the Poplar and
Greenwich Ferry Act of 1812. Apart from serving
local trade and industry around Millwall, one of
the principal aims of the new branch line was to
link Fenchurch Street with these ferries, and the
name allotted to the branch terminus was 'North
Greenwich'.

The line was jointly promoted by the LBR and
the Millwall Canal Company, the latter of which
was then actively engaged in the completion of
its new Millwall Docks. The route was to have a
total length of 1mile 49chains, and have two
intermediate stations.

The Millwall Canal Company was fortunate in
having a general manager whose opposite number on the Great Eastern Railway was his broth-
er, and therefore the two organisations were on
the best of terms. However, the same could not
be said of the relationship between the railway
and the East & West India Docks Company,
which saw the line as a threat to its livelihood.
During planning stages the directors made
numerous technical objections about the line's
construction, but basically, the main complaint
was that its existence would give the rival
Millwall Company a right of way over its own
property. Eventually however, after much argu-
ing and the intervention of an arbitrator, the
opposition was dropped from 21st March 1865,
when the bodies concerned finally reached an
agreement regarding the line's operation. This
meant that sections of track which passed
through dock premises would in fact be owned
by the relevant authorities, and that the trains
which travelled along them had to be hauled by
horses to avoid potential fire risks.

The process of sorting out the various objections hindered the construction of the line, and by
the end of 1867, only a short section between the
junction and the south side of the West India
Docks had been completed. The following year,
the period allowed for its building was extended
by Parliament until 1871, which was just as well
as the short section which linked the West India
and Millwall Docks actually took an amazing
four years to finish. By the time it opened to passenger traffic on 18th December 1871, the
Millwall Dock had been fully functional for over
three years, and its owners had changed their
name to the more appropriate Millwall Dock
Company.

At first, trains only operated as far as the station at Millwall Docks, but from 29th July 1872,
they were extended to North Greenwich.

Because of the various level crossings and frail
timber bridges, the line was basically a light railway, and for a while at least, the use of locomotives had to be ruled out for most of its length.

Despite its diminutive length, it was managed
by no less than three organisations, each of
whom was responsible for its own section of line.

The first 5 chains were retained by the LBR,
followed by 41 chains which were owned by the
East & West India Docks, and 52 chains belonging to the Millwall Docks. The final 31 chains
were again London & Blackwall property, and
consisted largely of a 682yard brick viaduct,
which crossed Manchester Road and Wharf
Road, a little short of the branch terminus in
Johnson Street.

The branch commenced at a new station
between West India Docks and Poplar, which
received the name 'Millwall Junction'. Although
this was technically correct in railway terms,

insomuch as it was indeed the junction for Millwall, it must have confused passengers, as the premises were actually situated to the south of Poplar High Street, and not, as its name implied, on the Isle of Dogs.

In 1874, the GER acquired the rights to operate the Greenwich ferries, and three years later erected a new pier adjacent to the branch terminus. After this was completed, through tickets were introduced which showed the landing stage on the opposite side of the Thames as 'South Greenwich'.

Originally, horses were used to haul the services between Millwall Junction and the boundary of the Millwall Dock Company, where a locomotive would take over for the final stretch into North Greenwich. This arrangement continued until August 1880, when, following sanction by the Board of Trade, steam engines were allowed to work throughout. The frail timber bridges were strengthened, but the branch was still subject to serious weight restrictions, so the locomotives employed had to be very small and light. To carry out the duties, three tiny 2-4-0Ts were ordered from the Leeds firm of Manning Wardle, and the first pair of these began operating on 23rd August 1880. Until this date, the trains had only worked between Monday and Saturday, but now the service could be improved, they ran on Sundays as well.

The line was largely used by workmen travelling to and from the docks, but was also busy during the football season. From 1885, the team then known as 'Millwall Rovers' began playing on a piece of waste ground in Glengall Road. When this was required for a dock extension in 1901, the club were obliged to move to a ground closer to North Greenwich station. On days when the team was playing 'At Home', the trains had to be strengthened to five coaches, which when full must have taxed the little engines to their limits. This happy state of affairs for the finances of the line ceased in 1910 however, when the Millwall Football Club moved their headquarters to New Cross, although by this time the fortunes of the branch were in decline anyway.

At one time it was estimated that there were 1,300,000 annual passenger journeys on the railway operated Greenwich ferry, but these ceased in the early twentieth century. A replacement foot tunnel was sanctioned in 1897, and opened on 4th August 1902. The GER naturally disapproved of this, but withdrew their objections after receiving £8,000 compensation, and the ferries ceased to operate two months later on 31st October.

The dock companies came under the control of the Port of London Authority in 1909, but the line remained a joint venture, with the Great Eastern retaining its existing sections.

On 28th December 1913, the Sunday trains were withdrawn, but otherwise the service continued much as before. In 1922, the PLA replaced the old Manning Wardle locomotives with three steam railmotors, which it had acquired second hand. Two of these had been built at Swindon in 1904 for the Great Western Railway, whilst the other originated on the Port Talbot Railway in 1906. Their length made them very tight on curves, and because of this the facing points had to be fitted with 45ft locking bars. It took some time to make the necessary alterations so that these could run on the branch, and it is understood that in the meantime, passenger services were operated by small GER 0-4-0STs.

Although leased to the Great Eastern since 1866, the London & Blackwall remained nominally independent until the grouping of 1923, when it became part of the new London & North Eastern Railway. The North Greenwich branch continued in joint ownership however, with both the LNER and the PLA being responsible for its operation.

As with the line to Blackwall, the North Greenwich branch was set to close on 30th June 1926, but almost two months earlier, on 4th May, the early turn loco crew was turned back by pickets at the dock gates, and the service ceased there and then.

THE NORTH LONDON RAILWAY

The NLR, or to give its original title, the East & West India Docks & Birmingham Junction Railway, was authorised by Parliament in August 1846, and was intended to join the London & Birmingham Line near Camden with the docks at Poplar.

Although initially planned for freight traffic, a passenger service was provided from the outset, when trains began operating to and from Islington. Because the company had no London terminus of its own, an agreement was reached with the LBR whereby it could use Fenchurch Street, and it was the introduction of these trains in September 1850 which led to the demise of the unremunerative LBR service to Victoria Park & Bow.

The route was a success from the start, and was

soon extended westwards towards Camden. Almost immediately, it was dubbed 'The Camden Town Railway' by the contemporary press, and from 1st January 1853, its unwieldy official title was changed to the North London Railway.

From then on, the company entered into a period of prosperity, with traffic increasing at a very promising level, and various new extensions opening at its western end. There was also an intention to push passenger traffic along the NLR freight only line south of Bow, but although a station was constructed in Poplar High Street, it was never used.

In 1854, a line was opened to link the Eastern Counties Railway with the North London near Hackney Wick. Two years later, a station was brought into use west of the junction, and named Victoria Park.

Within a decade, congestion at Fenchurch Street was becoming acute, and it was obvious that the North London seriously needed a City terminus of its own. Therefore, in 1861, an Act was obtained to build a new line, which diverged from the original route near Kingsland, and terminated at Broad Street. This was known colloquially at the time as 'The Happy Afterthought', and it opened on 1st November 1865.

From Broad Street, the NLR headed north, and passed through Shoreditch and Haggerston before reaching Dalston Junction. Here it divided, with one section curving westward towards Camden, and the other leading round to Bow. There was no longer a real need to continue into Fenchurch Street, but the NLR did so until 1st January 1869, when the service, by now reduced to a shuttle, was handed over to the GER.

On 1st August 1866, the line south of Bow was finally brought into use for passenger traffic, although the unopened station in Poplar High Street was replaced by new premises in East India Dock Road.

From 1st September 1870, some NLR trains were extended beyond Poplar, and ran by way of a connecting curve to the LBR terminus at Blackwall. Here they would link with pleasure steamers to Margate and other resorts, but the demand for these waned over the next two decades, and the NLR service was cut back to Poplar from 1st July 1890.

Another useful connection on this eastern section of the NLR was a curve linking Bow with the LTSR line west of Bromley station, which opened in May 1869. This allowed through trains off the North London to reach destinations along the Thames estuary such as Southend, although it also hosted a local shuttle service between Bow and Plaistow.

The working relationship with the Great Eastern Railway was also very good, and interchange facilities between the two lines were provided at both Hackney and Bow stations during the late nineteenth century.

Sadly however, the prosperity was not destined to last, as with so many inner-suburban lines, the North London route to Poplar suffered badly from tramway competition, and eventually traffic declined.

World War 1 saw the closure of the Bow - Bromley spur, but the branch itself survived until the next great conflict, when it was badly mauled by German bombs, both during the 1940-41 Blitz, and later.

Eventually train services between Dalston Junction and Poplar were withdrawn from 15th May 1944, although the station ticket offices remained open to sell tickets which were valid on replacement buses. This arrangement ceased on 23rd April 1945, when the stations were officially closed.

Freight traffic continued, and the line remained busy during the 1950s, but a decline set in during the following decade, and an air of dereliction soon prevailed.

In May 1979, a new passenger service was introduced between Camden Road and North Woolwich, and this utilised some of the old Poplar branch. Freight trains on the section south of Victoria Park Junction eventually became very few and far between however, and this part of the route fell into complete disuse in the early 1980s.

NEW LIFE FOR OLD RAILWAYS

In December 1982, Government approval was received for the Docklands Light Railway, which was intended to serve new commercial developments around Poplar and the Isle of Dogs. The line would be of the type known as 'Light Rail Transit', and would employ vehicles similar to continental trams.

The initial railway would stretch from a terminus in the Minories, known as Tower Gateway, and head eastwards alongside the existing Fenchurch Street line until it reached Stepney East. Here it would diverge onto the old Blackwall branch, and utilise the original viaduct adjoining the Regents Canal Dock. A little beyond the site of the old West India Docks station, the tracks would split, with one heading south towards the Isle of Dogs, and the other eventually turning north through Poplar. The latter would utilise the trackbed of the former North London Railway as far as Bow, where a new steeply graded curving embankment would take it up to the level of the Great Eastern main line, which it would parallel on existing formation to Stratford.

The other branch, which subsequently served the vast office complex of Canary Wharf, was to be built largely on a new concrete structure, although its southern end was laid on the old Millwall Extension Railway embankment and viaduct. Its terminus, known as Island Gardens, occupied the northern part of the former North Greenwich station site, and passengers wishing to visit Greenwich could do do by using the 1902 foot tunnel.

The line was officially opened by HM The Queen on 30th July 1987, but public services were delayed for a few weeks, whilst various technical problems were overcome. Regular passengers were first carried on 31st August 1987, and three long-closed sections of East End railway were brought back into full public use. Since then the DLR has seen many changes, with extensions to Bank, Beckton and Lewisham being opened. The latter needed to pass beneath the river between Millwall and Greenwich, and as it was impossible to descend into tunnel from the old Millwall Extension Railway viaduct, this historic section of line was again closed. The viaduct however is a listed structure, and remains standing.

PASSENGER SERVICES

The initial service on the London & Blackwall Railway operated at approximately fifteen minute intervals, and remained little changed throughout its early years. By the early twentieth century, this was reduced to three trains an hour, but towards the end, there was little demand, and the services were invariably lightly loaded.

The North Greenwich branch was principally used by workmen travelling to and from the docks, and at busy times, trains could be formed of up to three coaches, which was probably the maximum comfortable load for the tiny locomotives employed. During off peak hours, the need was drastically reduced, and often a single carriage would suffice. The rather flimsy manner of the line's construction meant that there was never a through link with the City, and all passengers travelling to or from Fenchurch Street had to change at Millwall Junction.

As previously mentioned, the earliest trains of what later became the North London Railway used Fenchurch Street as their City terminus, so naturally those running between Dalston and Bow were referred to as 'up'. Rather strangely, this practice continued after the extension into Broad Street was opened in 1865, and the result must surely have seemed odd, even at the time. Trains from Broad Street to Poplar would be regarded as 'down' until they reached Dalston Junction, where they would be redesignated 'up'. Therefore passengers joining at any of the stations east of here, who wished to travel towards the City had to use the so-called 'down platform'. With this in mind, the relevant photograph captions in this album refer to either westbound or eastbound to avoid confusion!

In addition to trains travelling to Poplar, there were also services which came off the GER at Victoria Park. In this connection's early days, through services were operated which initially entailed detaching or attaching at the junction, but after 1866, the majority of GER services terminated at Victoria Park.

At Bow, Poplar line passengers could either change for Bromley on the LTSR, or else Fenchurch Street. The regular services using both these routes were latterly shuttles, with those into Fenchurch Street being operated by the GER from 1869 until withdrawal in 1892. Local trains onto the LTSR generally terminated in a bay at Plaistow, but through services were also operated, particularly during the summer months.

The passenger service reintroduced over the section between Stratford and Dalston Western Junction in 1979 initially used Camden Road as its western terminus, but with electrification, the trains were extended to Richmond.

The Docklands Light Railway operates to Lewisham, Beckton, and Stratford, although the latter can only be reached from central London by changing at Poplar, West India Quay or Canary Wharf.

This highly innovative line, is a worthy successor to the old London & Blackwall Railway, and there can be little doubt that the forward-looking LBR management of 1840 would have been delighted to know that their ingenious, if not always reliable system of cable haulage, would over a century and a half later be replaced by state-of-the-art driverless trains.

LIMEHOUSE (FORMERLY STEPNEY EAST)

1. We start our tour of East End branch lines looking east towards the junction at Stepney East in the 1930s. The station had opened as Stepney in August 1840, and was enlarged nine years later when the Blackwall Extension Railway to Bow was brought into use. In the years that followed, it was subject to various alterations, and was renamed Stepney East on 1st July 1923. In the distance, the Blackwall branch can be seen curving to the right of the signal box, whilst the route to Bow diverges out of the picture on the left. (British Rail)

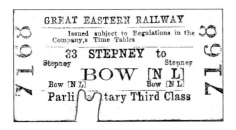

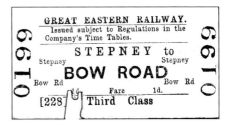

In this OS map of 1914, the station can be seen to the left of centre, with the original London & Blackwall line heading almost due east, and the route to Bow curving away to the north. The surrounding area of Stepney has a long history, which dates back to the eighth century AD, when it was known as Stebenhithe or Stibenhede. The street tramway is illustrated in the Middleton Press Album *Aldgate and Stepney Tramways*.

2. The Blackwall line platforms closed from 4th May 1926, and were largely demolished towards the end of the following decade, so photographs of them intact are extremely rare. In this view, the photographer was looking west towards the remains of the down side buildings, and has also recorded the signal box, which stood at the junction until 1961. The junction was severed in the 1950s, but a single track was retained as a siding until the following decade, being accessed from the opposite end. It was last used around 1962, and was lifted a few years later. Other views of this station can be found in the companion album *Fenchurch Street-Barking*. (R.A.P. Cogger)

3. In 1984, work commenced on rehabilitating the old Blackwall branch viaduct in readiness for its incorporation in the Docklands Light Railway. A new station, called Limehouse, was erected where the former branch platforms once stood, and the existing British Rail station had its name changed from Stepney East to Limehouse on 11th May 1987. Here DLR Class P86 vehicle No 04 pauses at the up side whilst operating a trial trip to Tower Gateway late on a Summer evening shortly before public services began at the end of August 1987. (J.E. Connor)

LIMEHOUSE JUNCTION

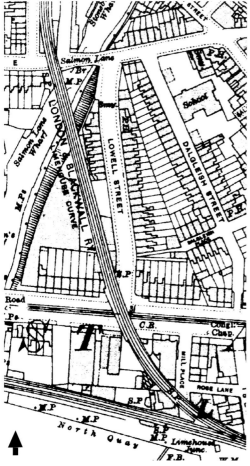

4. In April 1880, a new line was opened to link the original London & Blackwall route at Limehouse Junction with the Blackwall Extension Railway at Salmons Lane. It was primarily intended for freight traffic, but also carried passenger services in 1880-81 and 1890-91. The photograph shows an enthusiasts' special headed by Class J69 0-6-0T No E8619, travelling from the Stepney direction on 14th April 1951, with the 1880 connection, or Limehouse Curve as it became known, just visible to the right. The tall brick building behind the locomotive is an accumulator tower built in 1852 to provide hydraulic power within the Regents Canal Dock, whilst between the diverging lines can be seen *The Volunteer* public house. Part of this was built within the viaduct arches, and glasses hanging behind the bar would rattle alarmingly every time a train passed overhead! (E.R. Wethersett)

This 1914 map shows Limehouse Junction at the bottom right, with the 1880 connection to the Blackwall Extension Railway curving towards the north-west.

LIMEHOUSE

5. Limehouse was the first station east of Stepney on the Blackwall branch, and opened with the line in 1840. It was subsequently rebuilt, and received various alterations over the years. Here, the photographer was standing at the London end in July 1921, looking towards the stairway which provided access to and from the street level building. (British Rail)

6. Moving further along the same platform, we can see that the awning was fairly short and only offered shelter for passengers waiting at the west end of the station. In the background stands St. Anne's Parish Church, which was built to the design of Nicholas Hawksmoor, a pupil of Sir Christopher Wren, in 1712. (British Rail)

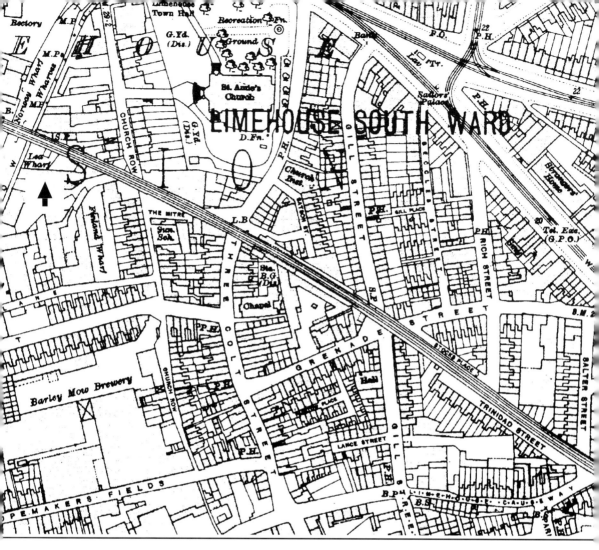

This section of the 1914 Ordnance Survey map shows the station near the centre, with its entrance in Three Colt Street, and its two platforms at viaduct level. Immediately north of the line is St. Anne's Parish Church, whilst to the south stands the Barley Mow Brewery. This was owned by the local company of Taylor Walker, which was founded in 1730, and latterly produced an ale known as *Main Line*, enjoyed by generations of East Enders. The business was acquired by Ind Coope Ltd in 1959, and the brewery subsequently demolished for redevelopment. The name 'Limehouse' originates from the thirteenth century Lymostes, which were kilns erected in the area for burning lime.

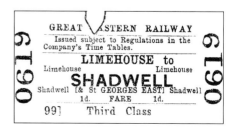

7. The street level entrance was located on the north side of the viaduct, and was again subject to rebuilding since opening in 1840. The wooden platforms and associated buildings were demolished in 1929, three years after closure, but the more substantial structure seen here in 1967 survived, and for many years was used as factory premises. (J.E. Connor)

8. When the line was reopened as part of the Docklands Light Railway in 1987, the old station at Limehouse remained closed. Here, a Class P86 vehicle hurries past the site en-route to Tower Gateway soon after the commencement of public services. The former street level entrance can be seen to the left, whilst the Regents Canal Dock accumulator tower is just visible in the distance on the right. (J.E. Connor)

9. The demand for local housing in the area was so acute that four dwellings were built within the viaduct arches on the north side of Trinidad Street, Limehouse. This October 1936 view shows their frontages, and it is understood that small gardens were provided at the rear. (British Rail)

10. One of the new stations provided for the Docklands Light Railway was Westferry, which is seen here shortly after opening, with Class P86 vehicle No 06 standing at the down platform. As its name implies, the premises are located in West Ferry Road, a short distance from the London end of the earlier station at West India Docks. (J.E. Connor)

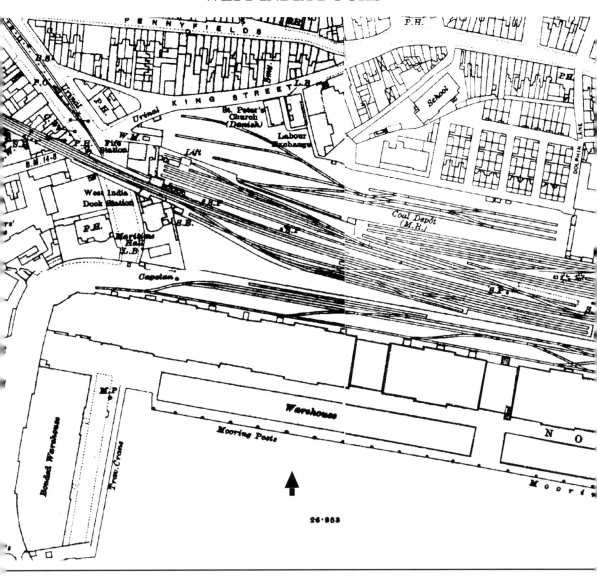

The entrance to West India Docks station was on the east side of West India Dock Road. As can be seen from this 1914 Ordnance Survey map, there were also extensive yards and sidings in the area, some of which provided a direct connection with the docks, whilst others served the Midland Railway coal depot.

Work on building the docks themselves commenced in July 1800, when William Pitt ceremonially laid the first stone. They were the first wet docks to be constructed within the Pool of London, and covered an area of 242 acres. The first section opened in August 1802, and the complex was subsequently enlarged. Originally, there were two docks, with one for imports and one for exports.

The street known as Pennyfields, shown to the north of the line was once the centre of London's original 'China Town'; as from the 1890s, a number of Chinese immigrants began to settle in the district, and eventually started various businesses, including the capital's first Chinese restaurants.

This contemporary engraving of West India Docks shows what is understood to be the standard design originally used by the LBR for its intermediate stations. (The Literary World 11.7.1840.)

11. In common with Stepney and Limehouse, the station underwent rebuilding, and various alterations during its existence. It is believed to have been demolished between 1931 and 1934, and nothing remained by the time this view was taken in 1967. We are looking west along the site of the platforms, with the public house known as *Charlie Brown's* on the right. Charlie Brown was the licensee of the premises until his death in 1932, and embellished his bars with curios such as old weapons and opium pipes, which had been traded for drink by seamen who had acquired them during their travels. The pub was demolished in the 1980s. (J.E. Connor)

12. To work the sidings of its West India Docks coal depot, the Midland Railway introduced a tiny four wheeled shunter in 1914, which was later known as B.E.L. (*Battery Electric Locomotive*) No. 1. The yard had track at both street and viaduct level, and the great advantage that B.E.L. No. 1 had over a steam locomotive was that it was small and light enough to be transported between both of these by means of a wagon hoist. Here it is seen on 15th May 1956, on the occasion of a visit by an enthusiasts special. In the background stands the grim bulk of a former workhouse which faced onto the south side of Poplar High Street, but was then in its early stages of demolition. (B.P. Pask)

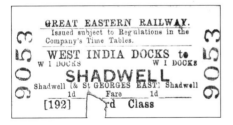

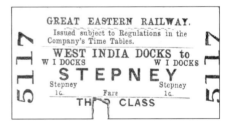

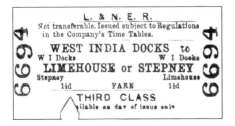

13. This view, taken on 14th April 1951, shows former North London Railway 0-6-0T No. 58861 shunting the yard near West India Docks. The tracks of this stretched from the Midland coal depot in the west to Harrow Lane in the east. The extensive complex of sidings at Harrow Lane originated in 1866, and were intended for transfer traffic between the North London and London & Blackwall Railways. (Dr. E. A. Course)

14. On the down side of the LBR, a little to the east of view No.13, stood Bank signal box, where heavily loaded trains comprising thirty-five or forty-five banana vans would sometimes wait for a banking engine before continuing their climb up to viaduct level. Here, the box is seen from a passing enthusiasts' special, in a photograph believed to date from 1960. (R. Blencowe Collection)

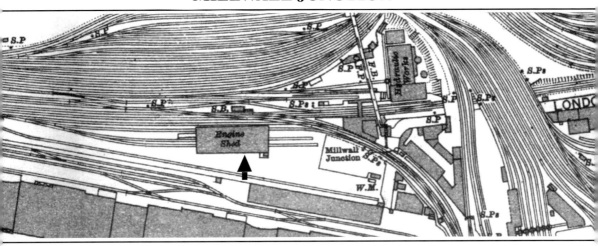

This map of 1914 shows us the vast complex of trackwork around Millwall Junction. The station itself is seen near the centre, with two platform faces serving the Blackwall line, and one for North Greenwich branch trains. The booking office was located on the platform, and was reached by means of a long footbridge, which led from the south end of Harrow Lane. Near the station stood a small three-road locomotive depot, which opened in 1871 to replace earlier facilities at Blackwall, and may have been converted from an existing goods shed. Harrow Lane yard was located on the opposite side of the formation, whilst the tracks shown passing over the Blackwall route to the right, originated from the North London line, and led to various riverside goods depots.

15.   A fine view of the station taken in 1936, when it was still substantially intact, despite ten years of closure. The double track Blackwall line is to the left, whilst the North Greenwich branch veers off on the right, and encounters the first of many gated crossings which abounded in the docks. Millwall Junction opened on 18th December 1871, but was rebuilt into the form seen here at a cost of £1,300 in 1888. (British Rail)

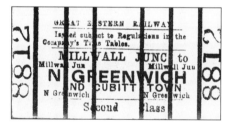

GREAT EASTERN RAILWAY.
Issued subject to Regulations in the
Company's Time Tables.

MILLWALL JUNCTION to
Millwall Jun   Millwall Jun

STEPNEY

Stepney   Stepney
1d.   Fare   1d.
2]   **Third Class**

1507   1507

16. A train for North Greenwich awaits departure from Millwall Junction, behind Manning Wardle 2-4-0T No 6, around 1910. These locomotives were the smallest ever employed on a British standard gauge passenger line, and bore a strong similarity to a pair of 0-6-0Ts built by the same company and delivered to the 3ft gauge Ravenglass & Eskdale Railway in 1875-76. (Lens of Sutton)

GREAT EASTERN RAILWAY
Issued subject to Regulations in the
Company's Time Tables.

MILLWALL JUNC to
Millwall Jun   Millwall Jun

N GREENWICH
AND CUBITT TOWN
N Greenwich   N Greenwich

Second Class

8812   8812

17. Staff line up on the branch platform at Millwall Junction beside one of the ex-GWR steam railmotors in the 1920s. Three of these units were acquired, and all had to be specially reduced in weight. Nevertheless, they still proved too heavy, and many of the line's bridges had to be strengthened before they were allowed to operate. (Island History Society)

18. Looking east in February 1950, it is apparent that a certain amount of demolition had taken place, although the platforms and main building were still standing. The footbridge which provided passenger access from Harrow Lane came in from the left, and led in turn to dock premises on the opposite side of the line. The trackwork appears to have been little altered since the 1930s, and was still very much in use for freight traffic. The building immediately behind the bridge was the hydraulic accumulator tower used to supply power for the nearby North London Railway goods depot, whilst the track curving towards the photographer in the left foreground provided a connection with the yard at Harrow Lane. (R.A.P. Cogger)

19. A member of staff leans against the former up Blackwall line platform as ex-NLR 0-6-0T No. 58859 stands at the station with the Locomotive Club of Great Britain Poplar & Edgware railtour on 5th May 1956. (K. Butcher)

20. From the start of the North Greenwich branch, we look north-west towards the disused station in the 1950s, and see the footbridge which led across the line into the adjoining docks. (Stephenson Locomotive Society)

21. A short distance from the North Greenwich end of the branch platform stood the rather confusingly named West India Docks signal box. This is viewed in the 1950s, with the line from the former station coming in from the left, and a track serving the docks disappearing behind securely closed gates nearby. The box remained standing, albeit derelict, into the mid-1970s. (Stephenson Locomotive Society)

22. On Saturday 21st October 1967, the Railway Correspondence & Travel Society operated a special train around various non-passenger lines in east London and Essex. Here it is seen standing behind the former down platform at Millwall Junction, on the line linking Poplar NLR with Harrow Lane sidings. The station building was demolished about two years earlier, but the footbridge which once served it was still in position above the tracks. The whole area once occupied by the station and yards was cleared in the 1980s, and now accommodates a main road, and the Docklands Light Railway, although the latter is on a completely new formation, and does not utilise the earlier trackbed at this location. (J.E. Connor)

FENCHURCH STREET, STEPNEY (EAST), POPLAR, and BLACKWALL.—L. & N. E.

Down—Week Days only.

Miles.		First.		Last.	
		mrn		aft	
	Fenchurch Street .....dep.	6 42	....	7e56	....
½	Leman Street.........{East	6 44	....	7e58	....
1	Shadwell and St. George's	6 46	....	8e0	....
1½	Stepney (East)	6 48	....	8e3	....
2¼	Limehouse	6 51	....	8e5	....
2½	West India Docks	6 52	....	8e6	....
3	Millwall Junction 765.....	6 54	....	8e8	....
3¼	Poplar....................	6 56	....	8e10	....
3½	Blackwall ....arr.	6 58	....	8e12	....

From Fenchurch Street to Blackwall at 6 42, 7 10, 7 26, 7 41, 7 53, 8 13, 8 31, 8 53, 9 10, 9 25, 9 43, 9 55, 10 11, 10 26, 10 40, 10 55, 11 11, 11 25, 11 40, and 11 54 mrn.; 12 10, 12e25, 12s32, 12e42, 12s52, 12e54, 1 10, 1 25, 1 40, 1 55, 2 12, 2 25, 2e39, 2 55, 3e12, 3e25, 3e40, 3e55, 4e9, 4e25, 4e38, 4e55, 5e7, 5e25, 5e38, 5e54, 6e10, 6e25, 6e40, 6e55, 7e23, and 7e56 aft.

e Except Saturdays. s Saturdays only.

BLACKWALL, POPLAR, STEPNEY (EAST), and FENCHURCH STREET.—L. & N. E.

Up—Week Days only.

Miles.		First.			Last.	
		mrn			aft	
	Blackwall....................dep.	6 50	....	....	8e5	....
¼	Poplar	6 51	....	....	8e6	....
½	Millwall Junction 765........	6 53	....	....	8e8	....
1	West India Docks	6 55	....	....	8e10	....
1¼	Limehouse	6 57	....	....	8e12	....
1½	Stepney (East) 786	6 59	....	....	8e14	....
2½	Shadwell and St. George's East.	7 2	....	....	8e17	....
3	Leman Street.....................	7 4	....	....	8e19	....
3½	Fenchurch Street ....arr.	7 6	....	....	8e21	....

From Blackwall to Fenchurch Street at 6 50, 7 5, 7 20, 7 32, 7 50, 8 2, 8 19, 8 43, 9 2, 9 20, 9 36, 9 50, 10 7, 10 20, 10 35, 10 50, 11 5, 11 20, 11 35, and 11 47 mrn.; 12 5, 12 18, 12e35, 12s39, 12e50, 12s59; 1e5, 1 20, 1 35, 1 50, 2 5, 2e20, 2 35, 2e50, 3 5, 3e20, 3e35, 3e49, 4e5, 4e18, 4e35, 4e48, 5e5, 5e18, 5e35, 5e50, 6e5, 6e20, 6e35, 7e4, 7e35, and 8e5 aft.

e Except Saturdays. s Saturdays only.

September 1925.

POPLAR

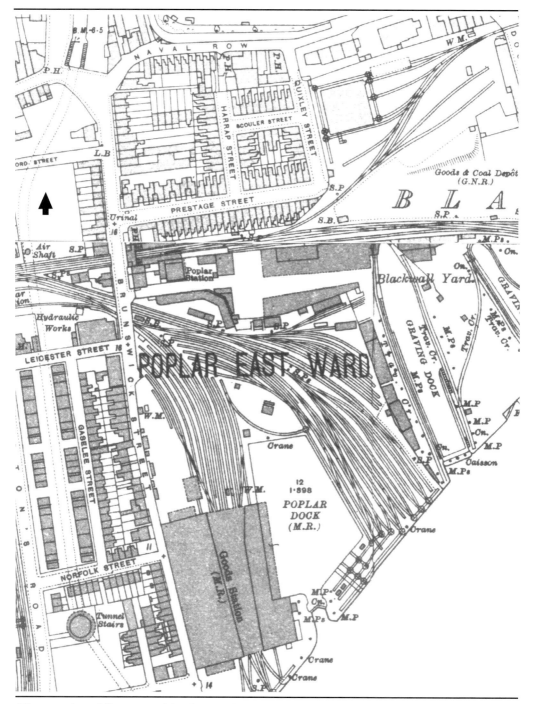

The complex of lines served by the London & Blackwall system at Poplar is clearly shown on this Ordnance Survey map of 1914. The passenger station can be seen on the west side of Brunswick Street, whilst goods depots belonging to the Great Northern and Midland Railways were located nearby.

23. Poplar Junction signal box was located immediately east of the bridge carrying Preston's Road, and controlled movements onto the Midland Railway dock branch. Here it is seen derelict and forlorn on 26th August 1961. (K. Butcher)

24. This earlier view dating from 26th July 1958 looks west from Blackwall Way (formerly Brunswick Street) towards Poplar Junction box and the Preston's Road bridge, whilst the track was in use for wagon storage. The red brick building on the left was erected by the Midland Railway in connection with its depot, and remained standing into the late 1960s. (A.E. Bennett)

25. Having passed beneath the Blackwall Way bridge, the Midland branch reached Poplar Dock signal box. Here this is seen on 26th July 1958, derelict, but still retaining its name-board. (A.E. Bennett)

26. The Midland Railway dock and goods depot opened on 1st December 1882, and occupied a large site adjoining the Thames. It was badly damaged during World War ll, but remained in use for a few more years. In January 1951 the premises became known as Poplar Dock Riverside, but by then their days were numbered, and traffic ceased after 4th May 1956. This view perfectly captures the desolate atmosphere of those final years, with a signal by the water's edge warning drivers not to shunt wagons into the river! (Dr. E.A. Course)

27.   The second Poplar station of c1845 remained in use until the Blackwall branch closed in 1926, although by this time it had been subject to various structural alterations. The booking office stood on Brunswick Street, but was demolished along with the platform awnings around 1936. In this February 1950 view we look west and see that a fragment of the down side stairway is visible to the right of the bridge, together with what is understood to have been a lamp or staff room adjoining it. In later days, only the former down line remained in place, and this was used to serve a scrapyard on the site of the old East India Dock goods depot. All surviving track was lifted by the 1970s, when the cutting was filled in, but traces of the up side stairway, complete with a short section of handrail remained visible into the following decade.   (R.A.P. Cogger)

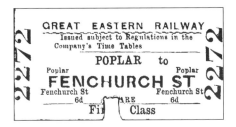

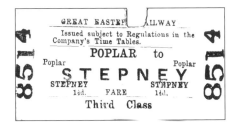

28. Just to the east of Poplar station stood Brunswick Junction signal box. This controlled movements in and out of the Blackwall and East India Dock goods depots, which lay on the north side of the passenger line, close to where the London & Blackwall Railway once had its locomotive and carriage depot. The depots, which were subsequently combined, officially ceased to function around 1961, although the warehouse was virtually destroyed during the Second World War. The Brunswick Junction signal box which is seen here on 26th July 1958 after closure, dated from 1906, and replaced an earlier structure which was located above the tracks. (A.E. Bennett)

The above Warrant must be presented for payment before 30th June, 1910.

LONDON AND BLACKWALL RAILWAY COMPANY.

No. **166**　　　*Secretary's Office, Fenchurch Street Terminus,*
(Chief Entrance: John Street, Crutched Friars, London, E.C.)

31st December, 1909.

Proprietor *Marion S Grieve & son*

I am desired to forward you the above Warrant for the Interest for the Half-year ending 31st December, 1909, *upon the Debenture Stock of this Company, of which you were registered as the Proprietor on the* 16th *instant, when the Transfer Books were closed, viz.:*

	£	s.	d.
On £ 1500 *Stock at* £4. 5s. *per cent. per annum*	31	17	6
Less Income Tax at 1/2 *in the £*	1	17	3
£	30	.	3

I hereby certify that the amount of Income Tax deducted from this Interest has been retained out of the rent payable by the Great Eastern Railway Company, as Lessees of this undertaking.

S. W. SAVAGE, Secretary.

N.B.—The Inland Revenue Department will receive this Statement as a Voucher on claiming repayment of Income Tax, and where the Proprietor is entitled to claim exemption or abatement, this portion of the Sheet must be preserved for the purpose.

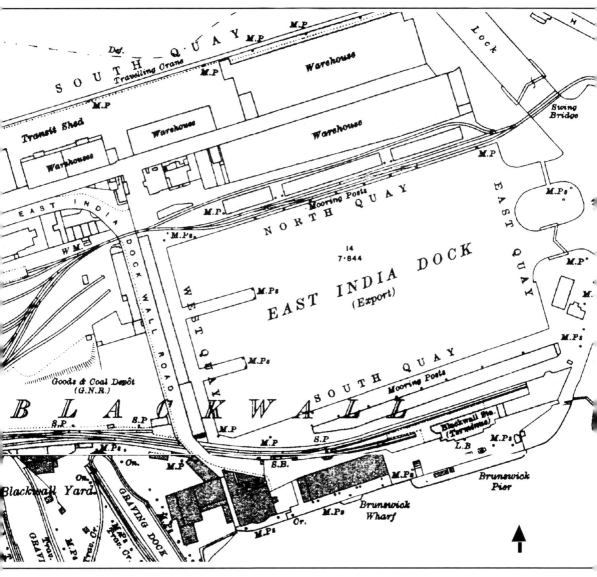

The terminus at Blackwall adjoined Brunswick Pier, and lay to the immediate south of the East India Export Dock. As built, it was fitted with a light iron overall roof, but this was replaced by awnings in 1906. In the line's early days, the nearby Brunswick Tavern was famed for its whitebait suppers, and passenger numbers were enhanced by those who wished to dine there. The Mirror magazine of 27th March 1841 described the tavern as *"a locality of high repute among the connoisseurs in gastronomy...it attracts to this neighbourhood the gourmand and the gourmet, to enjoy its peculiar delicacy of whitebait, with the luxurious accompaniment of cold punch."* The description then went on to say *"And thither, by aid of the Blackwall Railway, he may be wafted in less than 10 minutes!... Having arrived at the wharf, or pier, nothing can be more invigorating, or repellent of dyspepsia, than the river breeze to be enjoyed in a few turns along the esplanade."* Blackwall was obviously a popular destination, and the company's profits must have benefited from such excursion traffic.

29. The main building was designed by the architect William Tite, and was very imposing. Here we are looking south along Brunswick Pier, and see Blackwall station on the left, and the steamer *Braemar Castle* on the right, as she prepares to enter the East India Dock. (Commercial Postcard / J.E. Connor collection)

31. A member of the locomotive crew appears to be watching the photographer as Class J65 0-6-0T No 158 (running as a 2-4-0T) departs from Blackwall with the 1.35pm train to Fenchurch Street on 25th July 1925. (K.A.C.R. Nunn / LCGB Collection)

30.   This is a fine view of the station, looking towards the buffer stops, and although taken around ten years after closure, the premises appear to be still largely intact. Blackwall terminus survived World War ll, but was demolished in 1946 to provide a site for a new power station. (British Rail)

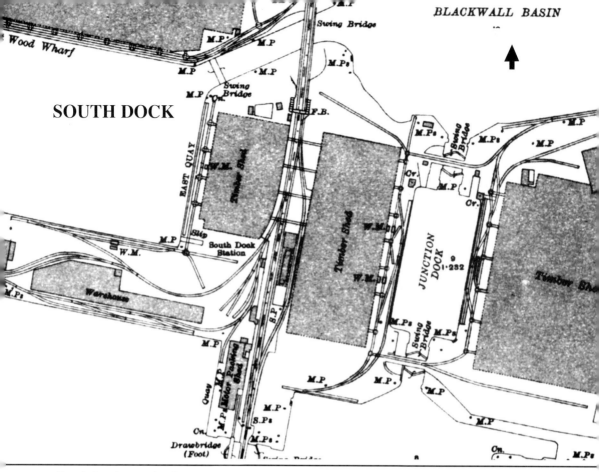

South Dock was the first station out of Millwall Junction on the North Greenwich branch, and as can be seen from the Ordnance Survey map of 1914, it was completely within the dock estate. It was opened with the first section of the line on 18th December 1871, and was provided with a passing loop together with office accommodation for the joint committee responsible for the line's operation.

32. The station comprised an island platform, although this is not obvious here as Manning Wardle 2-4-0T No. 6 pauses with a train for North Greenwich. Apart from the passing loop at South Dock, the passenger line was single throughout, although for much of its length it was paralleled by the tracks used for freight traffic, such as that visible on the right. (Lens of Sutton)

OUR LOCAL EXPRESS
Poplar to Millwall
and back same day

A picture postcard dated 1914, which lampooned the service on the North Greenwich branch. Cards carrying the same illustration were produced to satirise various rural lines, but few London routes seem to have been featured. (J.E. Connor Collection)

MILLWALL DOCKS

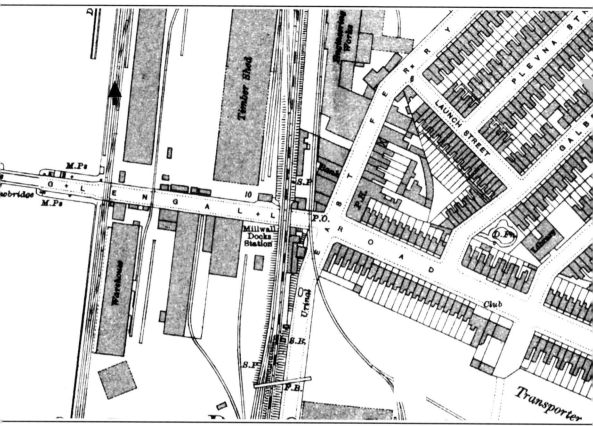

Sited to the south of Glengall Road, this station served part of Cubitt Town, in addition to the dock which provided its name. It was used as the branch terminus until the line was extended to North Greenwich on 29th July 1872. The Ordnance Survey map of 1914 shows both the North Greenwich branch which stretched virtually north - south for much of its length, and part of the internal system of dock lines surrounding it.

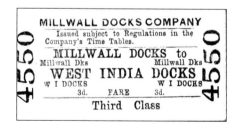

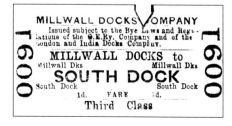

33. Looking north along East Ferry Road, we see the wooden platform and buildings perched on embankment. Passenger access was by means of the stairs visible at the far end, which led from Glengall Road to the booking office which was up above. Of the three stations on the branch, only Millwall Docks is thought to have issued platform tickets, although why this should be is unknown. (Lens of Sutton)

34. One of the little Manning Wardle 2-4-0Ts brings a train for North Greenwich into Millwall Docks station, sometime in the first decade of the twentieth century. The track seen on the left was for freight traffic only. (Lens of Sutton)

MUDCHUTE

35. The DLR line to Island Gardens utilised part of the old Millwall Extension Railway formation, and constructed a station on the east side of East Ferry Road. This was originally to have been called Millwall Park, but by the time it opened in Summer 1987, it had been changed to Mudchute, to commemorate a pneumatic dredger which was installed nearby to overcome silting-up of the Millwall Docks in the 1880s. The section of line through Mudchute was abandoned from 9th January 1999 to facilitate work on a new DLR under-river extension to Lewisham, and the premises were demolished soon after. This view, looking north, shows two trains passing at the station in December 1998. (J.E. Connor)

£0.00 CHILD 00 . 00   000 04710

klands   Docklands   Doc

ed · Docklands Light Railway Limited · Docklands Light Railway Lim
ee other side · See other side · See other side · See other side ·

THE ROYAL OPENING 30th JULY 1987 MUDCHUTE STATION

36. At the southern end of the North Greenwich branch, the single track was carried on a 682 yard brick viaduct. In this view, one of the 2-4-0Ts heads a two-coach train towards Millwall Junction at an unknown date. Sadly, the original print has badly faded, but its incredible rarity meant it just had to be included! (Island History Society)

37. The viaduct lay abandoned from closure in 1926 until 1987, when it reopened as part of the DLR. Widening it would have been an extremely costly exercise, so the double track of the new line became single at the south end of Mudchute station. Here, a train is seen heading towards Island Gardens in December 1998. After closure the following month, the track was lifted, and the modern bridge visible on the right was demolished, therefore leaving the viaduct completely cut off from the railway network for the second time in its existence. (J.E. Connor)

NORTH GREENWICH & CUBITT TOWN

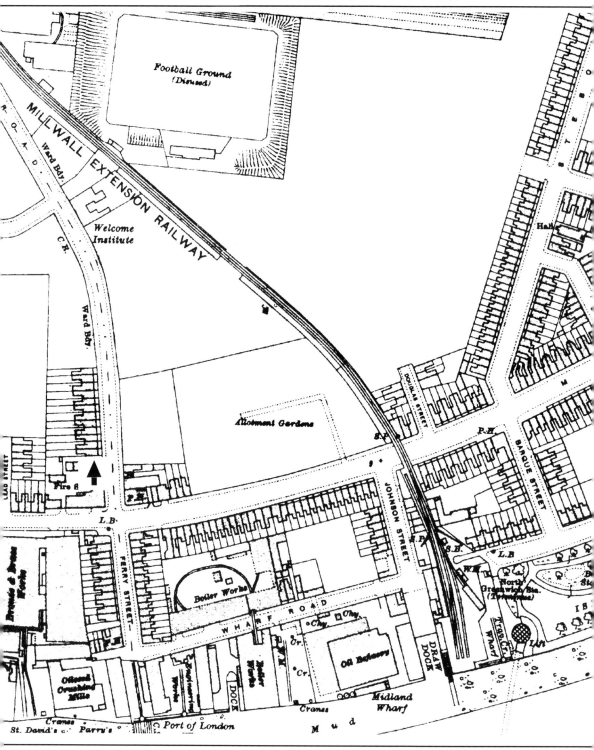

This OS map of 1913 shows North Greenwich station near the bottom right, with tracks branching off to serve a small engine shed and coaling stage. Nearby stands the entrance to the Greenwich foot tunnel, which opened on 4th August 1902, whilst near the top of the map can be seen the former Millwall football ground, which closed when the club moved to New Cross in 1910.

38. North Greenwich station was built largely of wood, and consisted of a single platform. In this view, taken on 14th September 1910, Manning Wardle 2-4-0T No. 6 has just arrived with the 3.53pm train from Millwall Junction, and prepares to run round. Unfortunately, the locomotive shed and servicing facilities were to the right of the photographer, and are not seen. The sloping covered way, just visible on the extreme left, led to the landing stage from which railway owned ferries operated to what the company referred to as 'South' Greenwich on the opposite bank of the Thames. These were withdrawn in October 1902, two months after the nearby foot tunnel was opened, and the pier was sold for other purposes in the following year. (K.A.C.R. Nunn / LCGB)

39. Looking east along West Ferry Road in April 1922, we see the bridge which was located just outside the terminus. The two men on the right are standing at the corner of Johnson Street (later Ferry Street), which led to the station entrance, whilst ahead of them, the cast iron gents and ancient lorry provide a delightful period touch. (British Rail)

40. The building stood on the east side of Johnson Street, and lay close to the bank of the Thames. The frontage was the only part of the station to be built of brick, and incorporated a course of stone in which the name was incised, together with the initials 'GER'. This view was taken after closure, and includes a structure to the right which is thought to have been part of the former ferry landing stage. (Lens of Sutton)

41. The building ended its days as a rowing club, but was demolished in 1969 when better premises were required. This view looks south along the sagging wooden platform, and dates from 1966. (J.E. Connor)

ISLAND GARDENS

42. In 1987, the Docklands Light Railway opened its Island Gardens terminus, which was located at the northern end of the former North Greenwich station site. As the DLR line south of Mudchute was carried on the existing 1872 viaduct, it had to be single, but at Island Gardens it splayed out to serve two platforms. These were intended for use by alternate trains, but when the trains were later strengthened by an extra vehicle, Platform One, which is seen on the right proved too short, and thereafter saw little traffic. A prominent feature of the station was the glass dome, which housed a stairway and liftshaft. This is visible just to the left of centre in our view, which was taken from the rear of a departing train on the first day of public service.

When the DLR decided to continue beneath the river to Lewisham, it was not possible to extend beyond this terminus, so a new line had to be constructed from a point south of Crossharbour & London Arena. This descended into cutting until it was low enough to pass under the Thames in a tunnel. It surfaced at Greenwich, then continued by way of Elverson Road to Lewisham. The last train into the old Island Gardens terminus ran in the small hours of Saturday 9th January 1999 to allow work on the new route to intensify. The extension, complete with replacement stations at Mudchute and Island Gardens opened on 20th November 1999. (J.E. Connor)

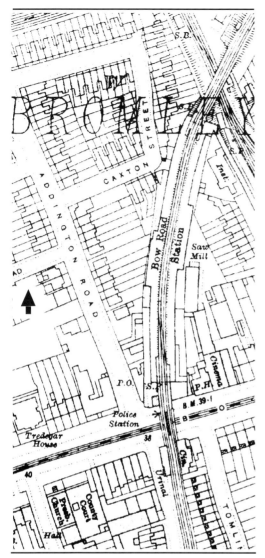

BOW ROAD

Before leaving the former London & Blackwall system, we will look at the section of line between Gas Factory Junction and Bow Junction. This linked the present Fenchurch Street-Barking and Liverpool Street-Ilford routes, and although not a 'branch' line as such, deserves to be included in this album.

As mentioned in the Historical Background, the line was opened by the London & Blackwall Extension Railway in 1849, but was initially beset with problems. A station was provided on the south side of Bow Road, and named Bow & Bromley, but this closed in September 1850. After laying derelict for over two decades, the GER decided that it should be rebuilt, and brought back into use. The necessary work was subsequently carried out, and the premises were opened on 1st October 1876, this time carrying the more appropriate title of 'Bow Road'.

In this form it remained until 4th April 1892, when it was replaced by a completely new station on the opposite side of the road. This was a costly exercise, but was carried out to afford an interchange with the nearby North London Railway station at Bow *(See 89-98)*, and once complete allowed an unremunerative shuttle service linking Bow NLR with Fenchurch Street to be withdrawn.

After closure, the 1876 station was used for a while as a coal office, and by an auctioneer, until 1912, when it was converted into a cinema. On this Ordnance Survey map of 1914, this is shown to the right of the line as 'Cin', just west of Tomlins Grove, although it closed soon after and subsequently disappeared.

The 1892 station can be clearly seen near the centre, whilst the line just visible at the bottom left corner is the Whitechapel & Bow Railway, opened in 1902 to link the LTSR at Campbell Road Junction with the Metropolitan District Railway. (See the Middleton Press *Fenchurch Street to Barking* album)

43. The 1892 station was built on a curve, and both platforms were provided with full length awnings. This 1942 photograph was taken from the Gas Factory Junction end, and shows that the up side stairway glazing had been removed due to war damage. Bow Road was closed on 21st April 1941, and remained out of use until after the hostilities had ended. (British Rail)

44. The station reopened briefly from 9th December 1946 until 6th December 1947, then closed again to allow various alterations, including the rationalisation of awnings. It was brought back to use on 6th October 1947 with separate canopy sections above the platform buildings, and the stairs which led to the street level building. This view is looking in the same direction as that reproduced above, and is thought to date from 1948. (A.W. Croughton/Lens of Sutton)

45. At the opposite end, two more stairways, similar in appearance to those leading from the street level building, provided access to Bow station on the North London Railway, which was situated in cutting below. This interchange facility, although deemed important enough to prompt the expensive resiting in 1892, eventually became little used, and was closed as a wartime economy measure in 1917, never to be reopened. This view was taken from the Stratford end, and dates from 1942. (British Rail)

46.   Despite being closed since 1917, the two interchange stairways apparently remained accessible until 1947, when they were sealed off. During the alterations of that year, the canopies were completely removed from this end, although from this photograph, looking towards Fenchurch Street around 1948, it seems that the stairway glazing was still more or less intact. (A.W. Croughton/Lens of Sutton)

47. Still at the Stratford end of the station, we see Class N7/2 0-6-2T No 9674 departing with a Fenchurch Street - Ilford train around 1948. (J.E. Connor Collection)

48. As part of a pre-war modernisation plan, the line between Fenchurch Street and Bow Junction was to be electrified, and provided with a shuttle service of electric trains, which would run to and from Stratford. Work on this scheme ground to a halt in the early 1940s, but resumed after hostilities ended. However, it was subsequently announced that the proposed shuttles were not to materialise, and the line through Bow Road would close instead. This view looks towards Stratford, and shows electrification work in its early stages on a foggy wet day in October 1949. (R.A.P. Cogger)

49.   In August 1949, Class N7/3 0-6-2T No 69733 pauses at Bow Road with an Ilford-Fenchurch Street train. The concrete platform lamp posts were erected during 1947, but their styling showed an affinity with the previous decade. At this time the station only had a few months to go, as permanent closure would come on 7th November 1949. (H.C. Casserley)

50.   Having taken the view reproduced above, the photographer turned his camera in the opposite direction, and recorded No 69733 passing the up side stairway as she continued her journey towards the City. (H.C. Casserley)

51. Despite closing to regular passenger traffic, it was decided to erect the overhead wiring after all, and use the Stratford-Fenchurch Street line for emergency diversions. The canopies at Bow Road were removed soon after closure, presumably in connection with electrification, but apart from these the station remained largely intact for many more years. This 1966 view looks towards Gas Factory Junction, and shows the stairways which once led to the North London Railway, after much of their glazing had disappeared. (J.E. Connor)

52. The platform buildings and lamp posts were demolished in October 1967, leaving just the two London-end stairways, which were used for storage. Here we stand between the tracks in 1968, and look towards Stratford. The station crossover, which appears in pictures 43, 44, 48 and 49 was removed in 1962. (I. Baker)

53.   The street level building received little alteration after closure, although from 1954 it was leased to the Power Group of Electrical Engineers, which manufactured neon lighting and illuminated perspex signs. This photograph was taken from the south side of Bow Road, and shows an up train re-routed into Fenchurch Street because of engineering works at its regular City terminus, Liverpool Street. The building was converted into a betting shop in January 1982, but despite undergoing some structural alterations and garish paint schemes it still retained much of its original character. (J.E. Connor)

54.   The line was included within the itinerary of an enthusiasts' special operated towards the end of 1981 to commemorate the passing of the Class 306 stock which, had it not been for the change of heart in 1949, would have worked the Fenchurch Street-Stratford shuttles. Here unit No 017 pauses at Bow Road, alongside the down side stairway, which at that time still retained its glazing, although its counterpart on the opposite platform had been re-roofed a little earlier. (J.E. Connor)

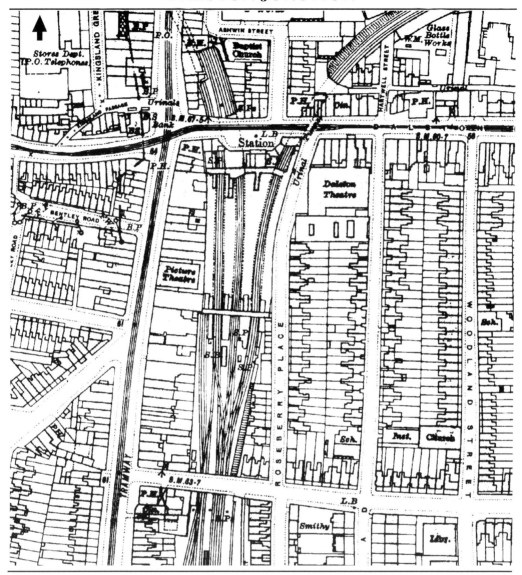

Moving away from the London & Blackwall system, we start our exploration of the North London Railway at Dalston Junction. This Ordnance Survey map of 1913 shows the station at the peak of its development, when it had platform faces serving all lines. The pair on the east side were used by Bow and Poplar trains, and this is the route which we will be following. The other platforms served the lines to Willesden and beyond, together with the spur onto the Great Northern near Canonbury. This section is featured in the Middleton Press *North London Line* album, together with views of the route between Dalston Junction and Broad Street.

The station's street level building was located on the south side of Dalston Lane, but there was also a supplementary entrance off Roseberry Place, which was referred to as the 'East Office'. Dalston Junction opened with the NLR City Extension to Broad Street on 1st November 1865, and replaced an earlier station known as Kingsland, which dated from 1850.

55. This is the view looking towards the south end of the station, some time in the early years of the twentieth century. The signal posts rose to a height of 86ft 6ins, and were specially constructed in 1886 to be clearly visible above the Forest Road bridge which is seen behind. To the right, a train from Poplar or Bow is making its way towards Broad Street, headed by one of the once ubiquitous outside cylinder NLR 4-4-0Ts. (J.E. Connor Collection)

56. Still south of the station we see 4-4-0T No. 33 departing bunker-first with a train off the Finsbury Park line. It has just passed beneath a footbridge, which latterly lost its covering, but survived in a derelict condition until the early 1960s. The signal box visible on the extreme left also proved to be long-lived, and was not removed until 1985. (J.E. Connor Collection)

57. This 1950 view looks south along the two platforms which were previously served by Poplar trains. Despite being disused for six years, a large sign still hung beneath the section of glazed roofing on the right and directed passengers towards the branch. The buildings seen here were all demolished by the early 1960s, and the track was lifted around 1966. The west side of the station, latterly reduced to two platforms, lingered on until the line into Broad Street closed on 30th June 1986. (British Rail)

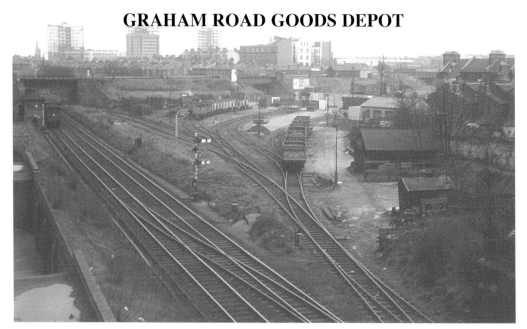

58. In May 1894, the Great Eastern Railway opened a goods depot at Graham Road, Hackney. This was reached by way of the NLR, and remained in use until 4th October 1965. This view, taken a few years before closure, looks east, and shows the North London Line to the left, Graham Road depot in the centre, and the former GER line from Bethnal Green towards Hackney Downs is carried on embankment and bridges in the background. (C.K. Hoser)

59. So that passengers using the North London Line still had direct service to the City after the demise of Broad Street, a single track spur was laid from a new junction at Navarino Road to the former GER, just north of London Fields station. This allowed trains from the Camden Road direction to reach Liverpool Street, and was opened on 30th June 1986, to coincide with the closure of Broad Street. For various reasons, the service was prone to cancellation, and it came as no surprise when it was withdrawn from 28th September 1992. The spur was retained for empty stock workings however, and is seen curving off to the right from the bridge carrying Navarino Road. (J.E. Connor)

HACKNEY CENTRAL

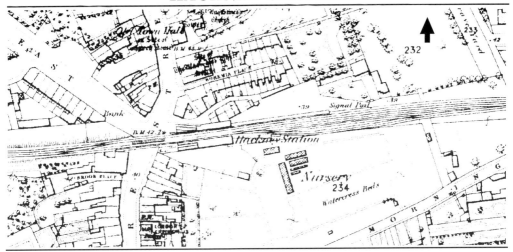

Hackney was one of the original stations between Islington and Bow, and opened with the line on 26th September 1850. It was sited to the east of Mare Street, and as is apparent from this Ordnance Survey map, its immediate surroundings were still fairly rural, even as late as 1870. In fact, a writer in the *Illustrated London News* of 15th November 1851 described his arrival by train and stated *"Looking leftward, we were somewhat puzzled at the appearance of several long ditches, or rather trenches, filled with running water, nearly covered with what we took to be weeds; but, upon enquiry, we found that this was one of the artificial streams for the continual growth of watercresses for the London market..."*

60. The only known photograph of the original Hackney station is as it appeared around 1870. During that year, the premises were resited to the west, and the earlier buildings were subsequently demolished to allow expansion of an adjoining coal depot. (London Borough of Hackney Archive)

61. The second station at Hackney was opened on 1st December 1870, as an immediate replacement for its predecessor, and stood on the west side of Mare Street. It featured a fine main building, designed by the architect Edwin Henry Horne, whose distinctive style became synonymous with NLR stations. Here the frontage is seen in 1965, twenty years after official closure. (J.E. Connor)

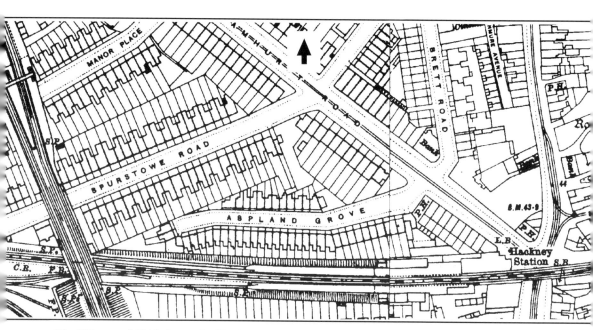

The OS map of 1913 shows the North London Railway at Hackney in relationship to the GER line through Hackney Downs. The NLR can be seen near the bottom, with a section of the Graham Road goods depot (See 58) just visible at the bottom left. A bridge carrying the Great Eastern crosses the NLR nearby, with Hackney Downs station almost immediately to its north.

62. On 16th January 1927, former NLR
4-4-0T No 2860 enters Hackney with a
train from Broad Street to Poplar. To the
left of the signal is the entrance to a covered way which was opened on 1st
December 1885 to provide interchange
facilities with Hackney Downs station
on the GER. One of these was located
either side of the formation, and paralleled the North London tracks until
reaching the Great Eastern, where stairways brought them to the height of the

bridge seen in the distance. Adjoining
this was a subsidiary booking office,
which issued both NLR and GER tickets.
The former showed the station of origin
as 'Hackney No 2', whilst the latter displayed 'Hackney Downs EO', on which
the initials indicated 'Exchange Office'.
The covered way was closed as a
wartime economy in 1917, but reopened
in 1923, and continued in use until services on the Poplar branch were withdrawn.   (H.C. Casserley)

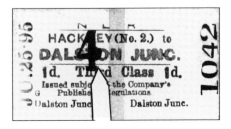

63. Looking eastwards in the 1930s, we see the upper storey of Edwin Horne's building, which adjoined the Poplar-bound platform. Immediately beyond this is the bridge over Mare Street, followed by the site of the long-demolished 1850 station. (Lens of Sutton)

64. Hackney station saw no more passenger trains after 15th May 1944, when the Broad Street-Poplar service was suspended due to enemy action. For a while the booking office remained open to sell tickets which were valid on special replacement buses, but this arrangement ceased from 23rd April 1945, when the station was officially closed. It was retained for freight traffic however, and in this view from February 1950, an ex-LMSR Class 3F 0-6-0T emerges from the mist with a train from the docks. The station was still largely intact at the time, although the platform lamps had been removed. (R.A.P. Cogger)

65. Demolition occurred piecemeal, and by the end of the 1960s, only Edwin Horne's main building remained intact. The derelict remains of the building on the other side was demolished during 1966, leaving just a length of rear wall which once helped support the canopy. Here, a class 37 Co-Co diesel locomotive rumbles past the broken, overgrown platforms with a train of tank wagons in 1968. (J.E. Connor)

66. With the re-introduction of passenger trains between Dalston Western Junction and Stratford in May 1979, it was announced that Hackney station would be rebuilt, and brought back into use. Prior to completion it was known as Mare Street, but when opened on 12th May 1980, the name had changed to Hackney Central. This view looks east and shows the new platforms under construction, with the remains of the 1870 NLR premises beyond them. Originally it was intended to bring E.H. Horne's building back into railway use, and its brickwork was cleaned accordingly. However, this was not to be, and although the structure was retained, a booking office was provided on the eastbound platform instead. (J.E. Connor)

Miles																							
0	**North Woolwich**	d	06 20	06 40	07 00	..	07 20	07 42	..	08 06	..	08 40	..	09 00	..	..	09 40	10 06	and at the same minutes past each hour until	15 40	..	16 20	..
¾	Silvertown	d	06 22	06 42	07 02	..	07 22	07 44	..	08 08	..	08 42	..	09 02	..	..	09 42	10 08		15 42	..	16 22	..
1¾	Custom House, Victoria Dock	d	06 26	06 46	07 06	..	07 26	07 48	..	08 12	08 36	08 46	..	09 06	09 36	..	09 46	10 12		15 46	16 06	16 26	..
3	Canning Town	d	06 29	06 49	07 09	..	07 29	07 51	..	08 15	08 39	08 49	..	09 09	09 39	..	09 49	10 15		15 49	16 09	16 29	..
3¾	West Ham §	d	06 32	06 52	07 12	..	07 32	07 54	..	08 18	08 42	08 52	..	09 12	09 42	..	09 52	10 18		15 52	16 12	16 32	..
4¾	**Stratford Low Level**	a	06 35	06 55	07 15	..	07 35	07 57	..	08 21	08 45	08 55	..	09 15	09 45	..	09 55	10 21		15 55	16 15	16 35	..
—		d	06 42	06 57	07 17	..	07 42	07 59	..	08 23	..	08 57	..	09 17	..	..	09 57	10 23		15 57	16 17	16 42	..
6	Wallis Road ¶	d	..	..	..	..	..	..	..	..	..	..	..	..	..	..	..	..		..	..	..	..
7½	Mare Street ¶	d	..	..	..	..	..	..	..	..	..	..	..	..	..	..	..	..		..	..	..	..
8¾	Canonbury 59	d	06 54	07 09	07 29	..	07 54	08 11	..	08 35	..	09 09	..	09 29	..	..	10 09	10 35		16 09	16 29	16 54	..
9¼	Highbury & Islington 59	d	06 56	07 11	07 31	..	07 56	08 13	..	08 37	..	09 11	..	09 31	..	..	10 11	10 37		16 11	16 31	16 56	..
9¾	Caledonian Road & Barnsbury 59	d	06 59	07 14	07 34	..	07 59	08 16	..	08 40	..	09 14	..	09 34	..	..	10 14	10 40		16 14	16 34	16 59	..
10¾	**Camden Road** 59	a	07 02	07 18	07 37	..	08 02	08 19	..	08 43	..	09 17	..	09 37	..	..	10 17	10 43		16 17	16 37	17 02	..

North Woolwich	d	16 40	17 00	17 20	..	17 42	18 02	..	18 26	18 46	..	19 06	19 40	..	20 06	20 40	..	21 06	21 40	..	..	..	..	..
Silvertown	d	16 42	17 02	17 22	..	17 44	18 04	..	18 28	18 48	..	19 08	19 42	..	20 08	20 42	..	21 08	21 42	..	..	..	..	..
Custom House, Victoria Dock	d	16 46	17 06	17 26	..	17 48	18 08	..	18 32	18 52	..	19 12	19 46	..	20 12	20 46	..	21 12	21 46	..	..	..	..	..
Canning Town	d	16 49	17 09	17 29	..	17 51	18 11	..	18 35	18 55	..	19 15	19 49	..	20 15	20 49	..	21 15	21 49	..	..	..	..	..
West Ham §	d	16 52	17 12	17 32	..	17 54	18 14	..	18 38	18 58	..	19 18	19 52	..	20 18	20 52	..	21 18	21 52	..	..	..	..	..
Stratford Low Level	a	16 55	17 15	17 35	..	17 57	18 17	..	18 41	19 01	..	19 21	19 55	..	20 21	20 55	..	21 21	21 55	..	..	..	..	..
	d	16 57	17 17	17 42	..	17 59	18 19	..	18 43	19 03	..	19 23	19 57	..	20 23	20 57	..	21 23	..	..	..	..	..	..
Wallis Road ¶	d	..	..	..	..	..	..	..	..	..	..	..	..	..	..	..	..	..	..	..	..	..	..	..
Mare Street ¶	d	..	..	..	..	..	..	..	..	..	..	..	..	..	..	..	..	..	..	..	..	..	..	..
Canonbury 59	d	17 09	17 29	17 54	..	18 11	18 31	..	18 55	19 15	..	19 35	20 09	..	20 35	21 09	..	21 35	..	..	..	..	..	..
Highbury & Islington 59	d	17 11	17 31	17 56	..	18 13	18 33	..	18 57	19 17	..	19 37	20 11	..	20 37	21 11	..	21 37	..	..	..	..	..	..
Caledonian Road & Barnsbury 59	d	17 14	17 34	17 59	..	18 16	18 36	..	19 00	19 20	..	19 40	20 14	..	20 40	21 14	..	21 40	..	..	..	..	..	..
Camden Road 59	a	17 18	17 37	18 02	..	18 19	18 39	..	19 03	19 23	..	19 43	20 17	..	20 43	21 17	..	21 43	..	..	..	..	..	..

For general notes see pages 2–4

A From Tottenham Hale dep. 06 28 (Table 21)
B From Tottenham Hale dep. 06 42 (Table 21)
C From Tottenham Hale dep. 15 43 (Table 21)
D From Tottenham Hale dep. 16 25 (Table 21)

¶ New Station to be opened from a date to be announced

§ WEST HAM STATION
The opening date of this station will be announced soon. Train times at other stations will apply before and after West Ham station opens

The Monday-Friday service of diesel trains between North Woolwich and Camden Road introduced in May 1979. This timetable is of particular interest as it shows 'Wallis Road' and 'Mare Street', which were the proposed names of the stations which subsequently opened as Hackney Wick and Hackney Central.

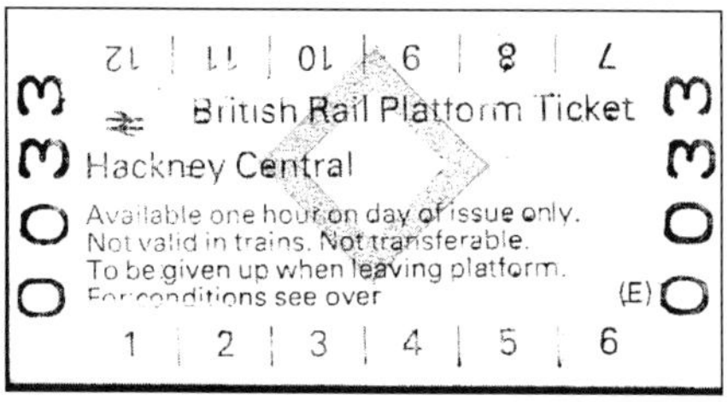

British Rail Platform Ticket
Hackney Central
Available one hour on day of issue only.
Not valid in trains. Not transferable.
To be given up when leaving platform.
For conditions see over
(E)
0033
0033
1 2 3 4 5 6
7 8 9 10 11 12

THE BROADSMAN
70000
Hackney Central

67. Preserved BR Standard Class 7 4-6-2 No. 70000 *Britannia* makes a fine sight on the morning of Saturday 23rd March 1996 as she passes Hackney Central with an enthusiasts' special train from Finsbury Park. (J.E. Connor)

68. Homerton opened on 1st October 1868, and had its entrance on the west side of Church Road, or Barnabas Road as it later became. It featured a fine and lofty street level building which bore all the hallmarks of the architect E.H. Horne, although the company minutes credit the design to Thomas Matthews, an NLR civil engineer. In its heyday, the station was extremely busy, and in 1898 when pull-bar machines for issuing workmen's tickets were provided in booking offices along the route, the demand at Homerton was so high that two had to be fitted whilst one apiece sufficed elsewhere. (British Rail)

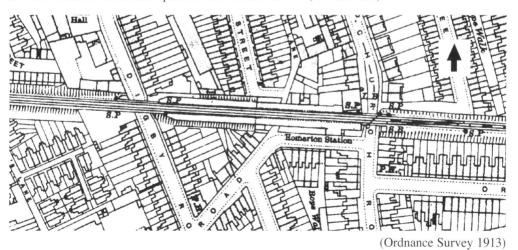

(Ordnance Survey 1913)

69. In addition to handling heavy passenger traffic, the NLR Poplar branch was used by numerous freight trains as they operated either to and from the docks or else onto the Great Eastern or London Tilbury & Southend systems by way of connecting lines at Victoria Park and Bow. Here, a Park 0-6-0T plods bunker first through Homerton with an eastbound train of coal wagons at an unknown date. The number carried on the left side lamp iron was once a familiar sight on locomotives working from Devons Road shed, and denoted the duty on which they were employed. (Locomotive & General Railway Photographs)

North London Railway
TO
HOMERTON

70. Poplar branch passenger traffic entered into a decline in the twentieth century, as passengers moved away from rail travel in favour of either buses or trams. Therefore it was perhaps inevitable that when its southern end was badly affected by enemy action during World War ll, the services would be withdrawn. By the time this photograph was taken in February 1950, it had been nearly six years since Homerton had witnessed its last passenger train, and the throngs of workmen who once lined the platforms had faded into the dim and distant past. (R.A.P. Cogger)

71. In time the demolition gang moved in, and swept most of the former station away. This view looks east in the late 1960s, and shows that although the buildings had virtually disappeared, a lower section of wall, complete with window ledges still survived, whilst the platforms lay broken and covered with foliage. (C. Mansell)

72. Although a new station was provided at Hackney Central in 1980, it was to be another five years before Homerton received similar treatment. The rebuilding was approved by the Greater London Council Transport Committee in January 1984, and work began soon after. Here, a two-car Cravens diesel multiple unit passes the construction work as it travels between Camden Road and Stratford. (J.E. Connor)

73. Of the original 1868 premises, the only item to be re-used was the passenger subway linking the platforms, as all else was totally new. The station opened on 13th May 1985, and was timed to coincide with the introduction of third rail electrification on the route. This opening day view looks east, as a former Southern Region 2-EPB unit pauses at the platform. Within a few years, the waiting shelters were replaced, partly through vandalism, and also because undesireables would sometimes lurk inside them and intimidate passengers using the station after dark. (L. Bolton)

HACKNEY WICK GOODS DEPOT

74. Hackney Wick depot was opened by the Great Northern Railway on 25th March 1877, and lay to the north of the NLR Poplar branch between Homerton and Victoria Park stations. It closed on 6th November 1967, but until the mid 1980s, the former entrance on the east side of Kenworthy Road retained a dark blue BR Eastern Region nameboard, as seen in this photograph. (J.E. Connor)

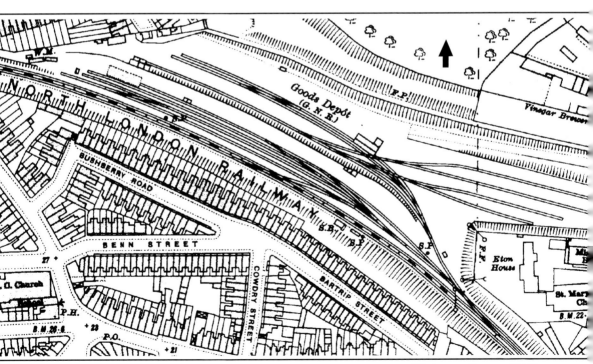

(Ordnance Survey 1913)

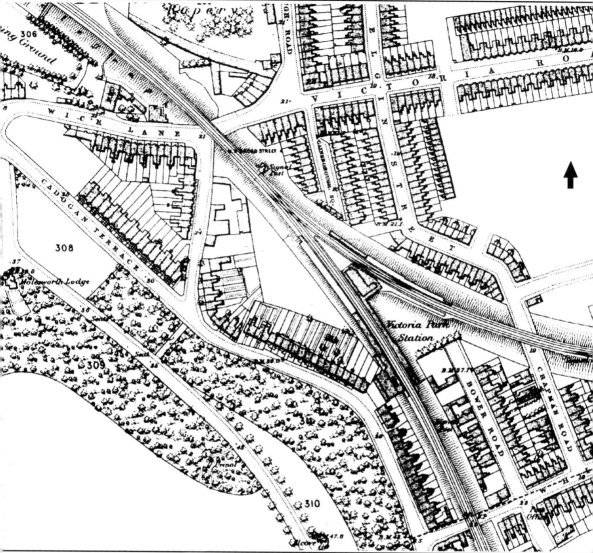

On 15th August 1854, the Eastern Counties Railway opened a line from Stratford to a junction with the NLR Poplar branch near Hackney Wick. Two years later, the North London constructed a station nearby, on the north side of what was then Wick Lane, and named it 'Victoria Park, Hackney Wick'. It consisted of two short platforms, initially without shelters, but waiting rooms and awnings were later constructed. It was opened for one day only on 29th May 1856 in connection with celebrations to mark the end of the Crimean War, but regular public services did not commence until 14th June of the same year. The facilities soon proved inadequate, and within a decade were replaced by larger premises, sited further east. The second station was located on the north-eastern side of Cadogan Terrace, and opened on 1st March 1866. It was provided with four platform faces, as shown on the 1870 Ordnance Survey map above, and although staffed by the NLR, also issued tickets for the Great Eastern Railway, which had absorbed the former Eastern Counties system in 1862.

75. The frontage onto Cadogan Terrace was imposing, although rather less ornate in its styling than stations later built by the NLR under the direction of E.H. Horne. This view looks across the road from one of the park gates, and was issued as a postcard by the well-known London company of Charles Martin in the early 1900s. (J.E. Connor Collection)

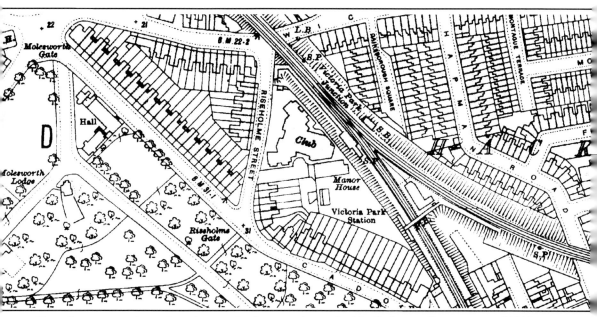

Over the years various alterations took place, as shown in this Ordnance Survey map of 1913. The eastbound platform on the Stratford branch was subsequently little used, and was removed during August 1895. The station continued to prosper however, and additional access was provided from Riseholme Street at its north-western end. This was referred to by the company as the 'Hackney Wick Entrance' and was shown on tickets as 'Victoria Park No 2'.

76. This view, which looks south-east from the signal box shows the station as it appeared in the 1930s. The footbridge was brought into use on 24th February 1891, but never stretched as far as the up Stratford line platform. Public access to this remained by means of a boarded crossing, but by then the platform was no longer in regular use, so the additional financial outlay of extending the bridge was not deemed worthwhile. (J.E. Connor Collection)

77. Here, the photographer was standing on the westbound North London side, and looking towards the junction. Although out of sight, the stairs from the booking hall surfaced to the left, and provided direct access to this platform, although passengers requiring trains to either Poplar or Stratford had to reach them by using the bridge. (J.E. Connor Collection)

78. Latterly, the Great Eastern service shuttled back and forth between Victoria Park and Stratford Market or Canning Town. From 1895, all GER trains used this platform, and the locomotive would run-round by means of the crossover seen here. This view, which is thought to date from the 1930s, also shows the station nameboard which advised passengers to "Change For The North London Line". For the convenience of those changing from the NLR to the GER without through bookings, tickets for certain local journeys were available at platform level, and these showed the issuing point as 'Victoria Park BS', with the initials denoting 'Barrier Series'. (J.E. Connor Collection)

79. A Park NLR 0-6-0T passes Victoria Park station, and heads towards Stratford with a freight train. (Locomotive & General Railway Photographs)

80. Victoria Park was the first station on the Poplar branch to close. The numbers using it had been in decline for some time, and from 11th July 1920, it was announced that the Riseholme Street entrance would only be open during the peaks. This closed completely after 29th January 1940, and from 1st November 1942, the LNER withdrew its Stratford services. At a meeting held the following year, it was stated that passenger figures had plummeted from 470,119 in 1929 to 13,785 in 1942, and that keeping it open, particularly during wartime, was simply not worthwhile. Total closure came on 8th November 1943, and partial demolition soon followed. This February 1950 photograph shows the Stratford line on the left, and the Poplar branch to the right. By this time, the awnings on the former GER side had gone, together with the footbridge, although the other buildings survived a little longer. The signal box remained in use until early 1961 when it was replaced by a new cabin between the two diverging routes. (R.A.P. Cogger)

81. Eventually, all that remained was the main building, which had been partially adapted for residential purposes. Here it is seen looking towards the junction in 1968, two years before its demolition. (J.E. Connor)

82.   With the run-down of the London Docks in the 1960s, freight traffic to and from Poplar fell into decline, but the line between Dalston Western Junction and Stratford remained as busy as ever. In this view, a Brush Type 2 A1A-A1A locomotive takes the former GER route, and passes the 1961 signal box. The junction points were removed on Sunday 5th May 1984, and the majority of track on the Poplar branch was subsequently lifted. The signal box at Victoria Park was used for a while by permanent way staff, but was largely demolished due to fire damage early in the following decade, leaving just its brick base. From May 1979, regular passenger trains have again passed Victoria Park, and although the premises have not been reinstated, a station was opened at Hackney Wick, a little closer to Stratford, on 12th May 1980.   (J.E. Connor)

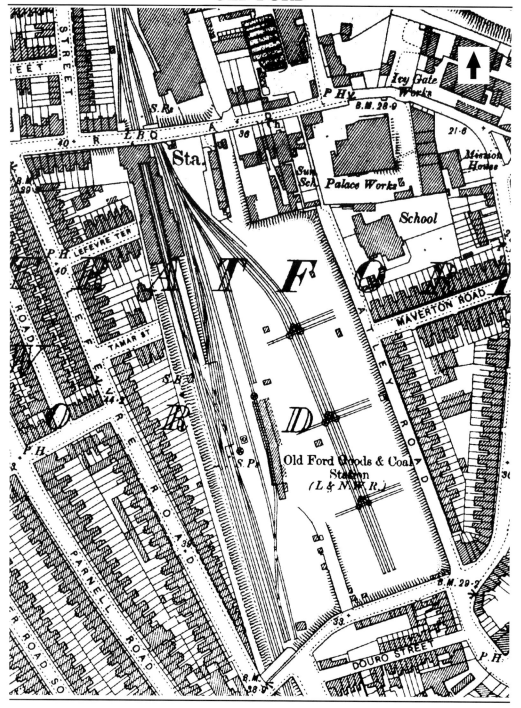

Old Ford station opened on 6th November 1867, and was located on the south side of Old Ford Road. In 1868, the NLR opened an adjoining goods depot, which was transferred into London & North Western Railway ownership two years later, and was subsequently enlarged. This map shows the extent of passenger and freight facilities in 1894.

83. The station was designed by engineer Thomas Matthews, and featured a fine street level building in the style of E.H. Horne, which can be seen to the right of this photograph from the early 1900s. Horne apparently had no formal architectural training, but learned his craft whilst working in France on the Paris-Rouen Railway. (Lens of Sutton)

84. The west end of the building displayed the legend 'North London Railway' in full, but because of restrictions imposed by the site, that to the east was abbreviated as shown here. Most NLR stations constructed between the 1860s and 1880s carried the company's name in this manner. The street level building at Old Ford was demolished in 1967. (J.S. Phillips)

85. The station saw off its last passenger train in 1944, but remained intact for some time after. This photograph, which was taken looking north in February 1950 includes a wooden frame to the left which is of the type used to display the LMSR 'hawkseye' type nameboards introduced in the 1930s. As far as is known, Old Ford was the only location on the Poplar branch where these could be found. (R.A.P. Cogger)

86. Over a decade later, the old station was little altered, although by now the buildings' days were numbered. Here, an English Electric Type 1 Bo-Bo locomotive is seen at the former westbound platform on 15th October 1962, as it prepares for a shunt move into the adjoining goods yard. (J.S. Phillips)

87. The same locomotive as seen in picture 86 is now in the process of crossing over, prior to entering the yard. The signal box on the right dated from 1900, and was the third cabin to serve Old Ford. It fell into disuse when the goods depot closed, having outlived the station's platform buildings which were demolished around 1963. (J.S. Phillips)

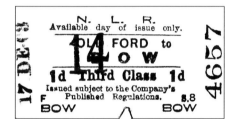

88. The goods depot remained nominally open until 6th November 1967, although towards the end traffic was virtually non-existent. Here we see part of the abandoned site from the west side of the line in the 1970s, with the largely demolished remains of the former eastbound passenger platform in the foreground. (C. Mansell)

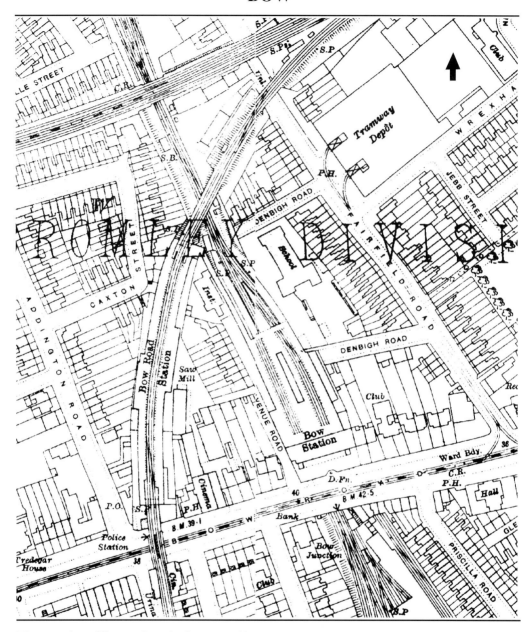

The complex of lines at Bow is shown on this Ordnance Survey map of 1914. The North London station appears to the right of centre, with its four platform faces, whilst Bow Road, which we have already looked at in photographs 43-54 is on the left.

Bow was one of the original NLR stations, and opened with the line in September 1850. At that time, it only comprised two platforms, but the advent of a connecting spur onto the London Tilbury & Southend Railway in 1869 hastened its enlargement. The tracks which are seen crossing from left to right at the top of this map constitute the GER main line, which is featured in the Middleton Press album *Liverpool Street to Ilford*. Lower right are the lines leading into Bow Works, which is shown more fully on the map adjacent to picture 62 in *Fenchurch Street to Barking*.

89. The station stood on the north side of Bow Road, adjoining the corner of Avenue Road, or Kit Kat Terrace as it later became. During the enlargement of 1869-1870, E.H. Horne provided it with this magnificent street level building, which included a large hall on its upper floor known as the Bow & Bromley Institute. This was used for various activities including lectures and classical concerts, and housed an extensive library. Although sponsored by two local organisations which were independent from the railway, the Institute was enthusiastically supported by the NLR, which encouraged its employees to take advantage of the facilities. The Gothic structure, looking a little like an Eleanor Cross, which is just visible behind the horse-drawn van is the Match Tax Testimonial Fountain erected in the station forecourt to the design of Rowland Plumbe in 1872. (British Rail)

90. Looking north along the Poplar line platforms we see 0-6-0Ts of NLR and LMSR origin pausing at the eastbound side, presumably whilst making a shunt move. The footbridge above the tracks led to the passageway which provided an interchange with Bow Road on the Blackwall Extension Railway. (Locomotive & General Railway Photographs)

91.   One of J.C. Park's NLR 0-6-0Ts brings a freight from the LTSR line through Bow station in the 1920s, carrying Devons Road duty number 49 on its top lamp iron. The two platform faces on the east side of the station were used by trains travelling by way of the Bow-Bromley spur, and lost their regular passenger traffic when the shuttle service to and from Plaistow was withdrawn on 1st January 1915. (Locomotive & General Railway Photographs)

92.   The interchange passageway closed in 1917, and the footbridge at the northern end of the station was subsequently demolished. This February 1950 photograph shows that the canopy on the eastbound Bromley line platform had also been removed, but otherwise, the premises had weathered their six years of total closure reasonably well. (R.A.P. Cogger)

93. This northwards view from February 1950 provides a clearer view of the buildings on the Bromley line platforms. A plastered section on the retaining wall near the centre of the photograph marks the site of the interchange footbridge stairs. (R.A.P. Cogger)

94. Here we are still looking north, but this time along the eastbound Poplar side as an ex-LMSR Jinty 0-6-0T passes over the Blackwall Extension Railway bridge, travelling towards Stratford with a freight train. (R.A.P. Cogger)

95. This is Bow Junction, which was located immediately south of the station. The original 1850 route towards Fenchurch Street diverges to the left, whilst the Poplar branch continues on the right. The building immediately behind the signal box formed the main entrance to Bow Works, where the NLR constructed its locomotives and rolling stock. The eastbound Poplar line platform can just be glimpsed beneath the bridge, whilst up above, E.H. Horne's imposing edifice appears to have had its upper windows boarded up. The view dates from February 1950. (R.A.P. Cogger)

96. After closure in 1911, the former Bow & Bromley Institute was leased out to the Salvation Army. It later became a billiards club, and finally a dance hall. In this guise, it was severely damaged by fire, and had to be demolished in January 1957, leaving the once-fine street level building reduced to what is seen here. In this form it served as a BR parcels depot until 1965, then stood derelict until November 1975 when it was knocked down. (J.S. Phillips)

97. The interchange footway was latterly used by a biscuit manufacturer, who converted it into a factory, although the working conditions must have been very cramped. This 1962 photograph shows its north end, with the rear wall of the exchange booking office, and the distinctive red brick stairways which led to the Stratford end of Bow Road station. (J.S. Phillips)

98. The platforms and associated buildings at Bow station were largely demolished in 1963, leaving just what is seen here. The train is an enthusiasts special which ran on 21st October 1967, and reversed at Bow before continuing into Fenchurch Street. The building on the left disappeared in November 1975, leaving just a section of the interchange footway as the final tangible reminder of what had once been an important, busy station. (J.E. Connor)

BOW CHURCH

99. To reach Stratford, the Docklands Light Railway utilised the formation of the former NLR between Poplar and Bow, then climbed by way of a new curving incline to the level of the ex-Great Eastern main line. This view, taken by kind permission of the DLR on the first day of public service, shows Class P86 vehicle No 04 passing the remains of the interchange footway, as it negotiates the single-line curve on its journey to Stratford. (J.E. Connor)

100. The DLR station at Bow Church is located close to the site of the old signal box seen in photograph No 95. This is its southbound platform as it appeared on 31st August 1987, having opened to the public earlier in the day. During 1999 its canopies were extended, and roofs fitted to the stairways. (J.E. Connor)

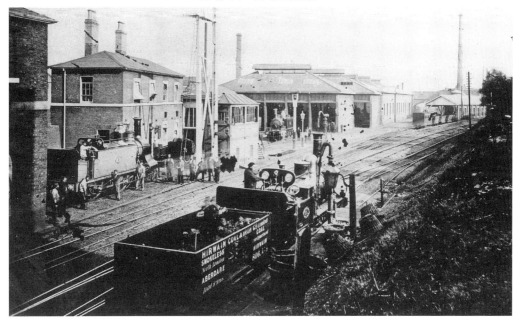

101. The NLR locomotive, carriage and wagon works was located to the south of Bow station. From company minutes it is apparent that a workshop existed in the vicinity since the line's early days, but the facilities were substantially enlarged under the direction of the eminent Limehouse-born engineer, William Adams in 1863. This view looks south, and shows the complex in its first decade. The works buildings are to the left, whilst what is thought to be the original locomotive running shed, can be seen in front of the large chimney on the right. (J.E. Connor Collection)

102. This is the locomotive erecting shop in the late 1890s, with various 4-4-0Ts and 0-6-0Ts undergoing repair. (M.J. Cox Collection)

103. On 6th November 1955, Class 3F 0-6-0T No 47483 passes Bow Junction signal box with a coal train from Poplar Docks to the gas works at Bow Common Lane. To reach this, the driver would continue into the station, then reverse and propel his wagons up the steeply graded connection to the Blackwall Extension Railway. This connection was used by the North London Railway for all its passenger services until the company opened its own City terminus at Broad Street in 1865. For a while, the NLR continued to operate a shuttle between Bow and Fenchurch Street, but this was taken over by the Great Eastern in 1869. In time the service began losing money, so it was withdrawn in April 1892 when it was effectively replaced by the new passenger interchange facilities linking Bow and Bow Road stations. The spur was retained as a freight link until 29th December 1967, when it was closed and subsequently lifted. (A.E. Bennett)

104.   Moving to the east end of the same overbridge, the photographer turned his camera southwards, and recorded this view of the abandoned spur which once linked Bow NLR with Bromley on the LTSR. This lost its regular passenger traffic in 1915, but was retained for diversions and excursions, as well as freight. It was officially abandoned in 1959, and soon lifted. A section of the works is visible to the right. (J.S. Phillips)

105. Bow Works was substantially enlarged in 1882, and the complex eventually covered an area of around thirty-three acres. Although the company remained nominally independent until 1922, an agreement was reached whereby the NLR would be worked by the London & North Western Railway from January 1909, and this arrangement resulted in a reorganisation at Bow, with consequent loss of jobs. In 1925 however, following the closure of Plaistow Works, the former NLR premises took on the responsibility of maintaining locomotives used on the LTSR section, so the facilities at Bow once again became fully employed. This situation carried on into the era of nationalisation, but as modernisation took hold, the workshops were no longer needed, so closure came in 1960. This view, which was taken from the parapet in Campbell Road, dates from 1966, and shows part of the premises a few months before demolition. (J.E. Connor)

106.   A former carriage shop lasted just long enough to witness the arrival of the Docklands Light Railway, even though by that time it had long been used by a scrap dealer. Here vehicle No. 02 has just travelled beneath the bridge carrying the LTSR line, and passes the building in 1987, not long before it was demolished. (J.E. Connor)

DEVONS ROAD LOCOMOTIVE DEPOT

107.   The locomotive depot at Devons Road was opened in 1882, and replaced earlier facilities which were removed when Bow Works was undergoing enlargement. It was erected under the instruction of the Locomotive Superintendent, J.C. Park, and stood on the east side of the Poplar branch. There were two sheds which backed onto the north bank of the Limehouse cut, and both of these contained ten roads. The coaling stage, which is seen here, sufficed for many years, but was replaced by a mechanical plant of standard LMSR design in the mid-1930s. (J.E. Connor Collection)

108. Both sheds were provided with northlight roofs, of a type favoured by the LNWR, and these provide an interesting backdrop for this portrait of inside cylinder 4-4-0T No.113. (K.A.C.R. Nunn / LCGB)

109. Until being replaced by LMSR Class 3F 0-6-0Ts, the majority of passenger trains on the Poplar branch were hauled by fine outside cylinder 4-4-0Ts, such as No. 2823, which was recorded outside the shed on 5th April 1924, carrying a Bow destination board. The shed furthest from the running lines was demolished in the mid-1930s, and the surviving building was fitted with a new louvre roof during the following decade. (H.C. Casserley)

110. Devons Road lost its last allocated steam locomotive on 25th August 1958, and became Britain's first diesel depot. In this form it lasted until 10th February 1964, when it was closed. The DLR opened a station nearby on 31st August 1987, and this view, which shows Class P86 vehicle No. 08 departing for Island Gardens, includes the former shed site, which had been cleared for redevelopment. (J.E. Connor)

SOUTH BROMLEY

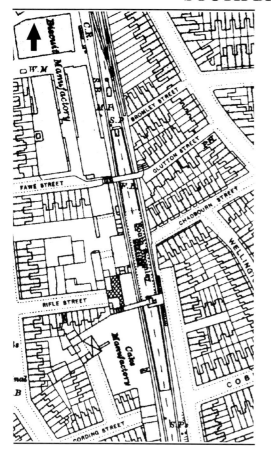

South Bromley was the last station to be built on the NLR Poplar branch, and opened on 1st September 1884. As little space was available, a single island platform was provided, with an entrance off Rifle Street. The Ordnance Survey map of 1914 shows the layout, with residential streets butting onto the east side of the formation, and factories on the west.

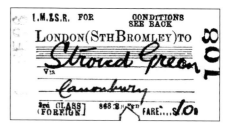

111. Photographs of the station are extremely rare, particularly those which show it intact. This view looks north along Railway Street in the 1930s, and includes the main building, which was positioned above the tracks, and was accessed by means of stairways. South Bromley was the scene of a mysterious fire in the small hours of May 1913, which was locally rumoured to have been started by Suffragettes, although this was never proven. (Locomotive & General Railway Photographs)

112. The fact that the station had to be fitted in amongst existing buildings is emphasised by its entrance at the east end of Rifle Street, which was an inconspicuous doorway alongside the premises of The Far Famed Cake Company. (Locomotive & General Railway Photographs)

113. Like so much of the East End, the area around South Bromley suffered dreadfully at the hands of Hitler's Luftwaffe, as can be seen in this view dating from July 1948, which shows the island platform on the right, completely devoid of buildings. During World War ll, the booking office was badly damaged by bombing, and tickets were latterly issued from a waiting room. To reach this, passengers had to cross the City-bound line under the watchful eye of a flagman. The ruined premises did not survive long after closure, as they are believed to have been largely demolished in 1947. (Dr. E.A. Course)

114. By February 1950, the remains of the station had been tidied up, and the coping stones had been placed in neat piles awaiting removal for use elsewhere. Although the former booking office had gone, the bridge which once supported it, and part of the covered way leading from the entrance in Rifle Street still survived. (R.A.P. Cogger)

115. By the early 1980s, freight traffic had become virtually non-existent, and the track had been singled. Occasionally, the branch would be visited by an enthusiasts' railtour, such as that seen passing the overgrown platform here. To the left, a chipped stone panel still displays the name of the long forgotten Far Famed Cake Company, although most of this disappeared following the opening of the Docklands Light Railway. DLR trains now pass the site, but all signs of South Bromley have been obliterated. The footbridge above the formation was erected as a public right of way between Fawe Street and Clutton Street, and was never part of the former station. (J.E. Connor)

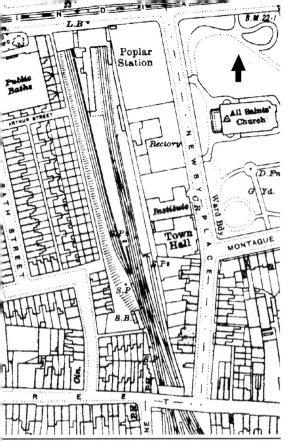

POPLAR
(EAST INDIA ROAD)
NOW ALL SAINT'S

The North London Railway station at Poplar carried the suffix 'East India Road' from opening on 1st August 1866. The reason for this was presumably to avoid confusion with the existing LBR Poplar station in Brunswick Street, but it may have been because at one time, the NLR had another station nearby. This was located to the south in Poplar High Street, and was constructed back in 1851. However, for various reasons it never opened, and was subsequently demolished. From the Ordnance Survey map of 1914 we can see the 1866 station with two platform faces for passenger traffic, and a dock on its west side. For most of its existence it was used as a terminus for trains from Broad Street, but from 1st September 1870 until 1st July 1890, certain services were extended by way of a spur to Blackwall, where connections could be made with pleasure steamers to Margate and other resorts.

116. The street level building stood on the south side of East India Dock Road, and displayed the various architectural features associated with NLR stations, although the styling was perhaps less elaborate than those which were opened later. This view dates from the 1930s, and shows the frontage after the LMS had obscured the original 'North London Railway Poplar Station' stone panels with two large wooden nameboards. (British Rail)

117. On a murky 16th January 1927, former North Staffordshire Railway 2-4-0T No 1451, painted in fully lined LMSR crimson lake livery stands at the station, having brought in a train from Broad Street. Five of this locomotive class had been transferred to Devons Road for working North London services, but they lacked the necessary power, and were soon returned to their native district. (H.C. Casserley)

118. Poplar East India Road was severely damaged during World War ll, and was largely demolished in March 1947. Here the abandoned platforms are seen from the brake van of a short goods train hauled by ex-NLR 0-6-0T No 58859 on 18th February 1956, as it passes Class 3F 0-6-0T No 47315 travelling in the opposite direction. (A.E. Bennett)

119. The old platforms were finally removed in the 1980s, and their site used to accommodate the DLR station at All Saints Chrisp St Market. This photograph was taken on the first day of public traffic, 31st August 1987, and looks north towards East India Dock Road. Although the majority of the earlier NLR premises have disappeared completely, a low section of wall, which once formed part of the street level frontage, still survived alongside the present station entrance in 1999. (J.E. Connor)

120. We end our tour of east London with this view of Class 3F 0-6-0T No 47315 hauling a goods train beneath Poplar High Street bridge, and passing Harrow Lane Goods Superintendent's Office. This large building, which dates from 1876-7, still stands, and although no longer used for railway purposes, was refurbished in the 1980s. (A.E. Bennett)

Middleton Press

Easebourne Lane, Midhurst, W Sussex. GU29 9AZ Tel: 01730 813169 Fax: 01730 812601
*If books are not available from your local transport stockist, order direct with cheque,
Visa or Mastercard, post free UK.*

BRANCH LINES
Branch Line to Allhallows
Branch Line to Alton
Branch Lines around Ascot
Branch Line to Ashburton
Branch Lines around Bodmin
Branch Line to Bude
Branch Lines around Canterbury
Branch Lines around Chard & Yeovil
Branch Line to Cheddar
Branch Lines around Cromer
Branch Lines to Effingham Junction
Branch Lines around Exmouth
Branch Line to Fairford
Branch Lines around Gosport
Branch Line to Hawkhurst
Branch Line to Hayling
Branch Lines to Horsham
Branch Lines around Huntingdon
Branch Line to Kingswear
Branch Lines to Launceston & Princetown
Branch Lines to Longmoor
Branch Line to Looe
Branch Line to Lyme Regis
Branch Lines around March
Branch Lines around Midhurst
Branch Line to Minehead
Branch Line to Moretonhampstead
Branch Lines to Newport (IOW)
Branch Line to Padstow
Branch Lines around Plymouth
Branch Lines to Seaton and Sidmouth
Branch Line to Selsey
Branch Lines around Sheerness
Branch Line to Shrewsbury
Branch Line to Swanage *updated*
Branch Line to Tenterden
Branch Lines to Torrington
Branch Lines to Tunbridge Wells
Branch Line to Upwell
Branch Lines around Weymouth
Branch Lines around Wimborne
Branch Lines around Wisbech

NARROW GAUGE BRANCH LINES
Branch Line to Lynton
Branch Lines around Portmadoc 1923-46
Branch Lines around Porthmadog 1954-94
Two-Foot Gauge Survivors
Romneyrail

SOUTH COAST RAILWAYS
Ashford to Dover
Bournemouth to Weymouth
Brighton to Eastbourne
Chichester to Portsmouth
Dover to Ramsgate
Eastbourne to Hastings
Hastings to Ashford
Portsmouth to Southampton
Southampton to Bournemouth
Worthing to Chichester

SOUTHERN MAIN LINES
Basingstoke to Salisbury
Bromley South to Rochester
Charing Cross to Orpington
Crawley to Littlehampton
Dartford to Sittingbourne
East Croydon to Three Bridges
Epsom to Horsham
Exeter to Barnstaple
Exeter to Tavistock

Faversham to Dover
London Bridge to East Croydon
Orpington to Tonbridge
Tonbridge to Hastings
Salisbury to Yeovil
Swanley to Ashford
Tavistock to Plymouth
Victoria to East Croydon
Waterloo to Windsor
Waterloo to Woking
Woking to Portsmouth
Woking to Southampton
Yeovil to Exeter

EASTERN MAIN LINES
Fenchurch Street to Barking
Liverpool Street to Ilford

WESTERN MAIN LINES
Paddington to Ealing

COUNTRY RAILWAY ROUTES
Andover to Southampton
Bath to Bristol
Bath to Evercreech Junction
Bournemouth to Evercreech Jn.
Burnham to Evercreech Junction
Croydon to East Grinstead
Didcot to Winchester
East Kent Light Railway
Fareham to Salisbury
Frome to Bristol
Guildford to Redhill
Porthmadog to Blaenau
Reading to Basingstoke
Reading to Guildford
Redhill to Ashford
Salisbury to Westbury
Stratford upon Avon to Cheltenham
Strood to Paddock Wood
Taunton to Barnstaple
Wenford Bridge to Fowey
Westbury to Bath
Woking to Alton
Yeovil to Dorchester

GREAT RAILWAY ERAS
Ashford from Steam to Eurostar
Clapham Junction 50 years of change
Festiniog in the Fifties
Festiniog in the Sixties
Isle of Wight Lines 50 years of change
Railways to Victory 1944-46
SECR Centenary album
Talyllyn 50 years of change

LONDON SUBURBAN RAILWAYS
Caterham and Tattenham Corner
Charing Cross to Dartford
Clapham Jn. to Beckenham Jn.
East London Line
Finsbury Park to Alexandra Palace
Kingston and Hounslow Loops
Lewisham to Dartford
Lines around Wimbledon
London Bridge to Addiscombe
Mitcham Junction Lines
North London Line
South London Line
West Croydon to Epsom
West London Line
Willesden Junction to Richmond
Wimbledon to Epsom

STEAMING THROUGH
Steaming through Cornwall
Steaming through Kent
Steaming through West Hants
Steaming through West Sussex

TRAMWAY CLASSICS
Aldgate & Stepney Tramways
Barnet & Finchley Tramways
Bath Tramways
Bournemouth & Poole Tramways
Brighton's Tramways
Camberwell & W.Norwood Tramways
Clapham & Streatham Tramways
Dover's Tramways
East Ham & West Ham Tramways
Edgware and Willesden Tramways
Eltham & Woolwich Tramways
Embankment & Waterloo Tramways
Enfield & Wood Green Tramways
Exeter & Taunton Tramways
Gosport & Horndean Tramways
Greenwich & Dartford Tramways
Hammersmith & Hounslow Tramways
Hampstead & Highgate Tramways
Hastings Tramways
Holborn & Finsbury Tramways
Ilford & Barking Tramways
Kingston & Wimbledon Tramways
Lewisham & Catford Tramways
Liverpool Tramways 1. Eastern Routes
Liverpool Tramways 2. Southern Routes
Maidstone & Chatham Tramways
North Kent Tramways
Portsmouth's Tramways
Reading Tramways
Seaton & Eastbourne Tramways
Shepherds Bush & Uxbridge Tramways
Southampton Tramways
Southend-on-sea Tramways
Southwark & Deptford Tramways
Stamford Hill Tramways
Thanet's Tramways
Twickenham & Kingston Tramways
Victoria & Lambeth Tramways
Waltham Cross & Edmonton Tramways
Walthamstow & Leyton Tramways
Wandsworth & Battersea Tramways

TROLLEYBUS CLASSICS
Croydon Trolleybuses
Bournemouth Trolleybuses
Hastings Trolleybuses
Maidstone Trolleybuses
Reading Trolleybuses
Woolwich & Dartford Trolleybuses

WATERWAY ALBUMS
Kent and East Sussex Waterways
London to Portsmouth Waterway
Surrey Waterways
West Sussex Waterways

MILITARY BOOKS and VIDEO
Battle over Portsmouth
Battle over Sussex 1940
Blitz over Sussex 1941-42
Bombers over Sussex 1943-45
Bognor at War
Military Defence of West Sussex
Secret Sussex Resistance
Sussex Home Guard
War on the Line
War on the Line VIDEO

OTHER BOOKS
Betwixt Petersfield & Midhurst
Changing Midhurst
East Grinstead Then & Now
Garraway Father & Son
Index to all Stations
South Eastern & Chatham Railways
London Chatham & Dover Railway